The Role of the Judiciary in the Violation of Human Rights in Ecuador

Six Case Studies

Researches:
Daniela Salazar Marin
Jaime Vintimilla Saldana
Jorge Zavala Egas
Fabricio Rubianes Morales
Carlos Manosalvas Silva
Rafael Paredes Corral
Sebastian Gonzalez
Pier Pigozzi

Presentation by Professor Douglass Cassel

Project Coordinator: James E Keeble

Typographic Design: Kiko Arocha
www.alexlib.com

Editorial Fund:
Interamerican Institute for Democracy
2100 Coral Way. Ste. 500
Miami, FL 33145
U.S.A.
Tel: (786) 409-4554
Fax: (786) 409-4576
www.intdemocratic.org
iid@intdemocratic.org

CONTENTS

INTRODUCTION -PURPOSE OF THESE CASE STUDIES

Recurring complaints of court rulings that violate human rights in the so-called states of the 21st-century socialism, i.e., Cuba, Venezuela, Ecuador, Bolivia and Nicaragua, and repeated complaints from citizens and the press of the judicialization of repression and criminalization of politics, have given rise to a serious crisis of judicial independence among these states—although they still strive to continue posing as democracies.

According to the third article of the Inter-American Democratic Charter, "respect for human rights and fundamental freedoms," the "exercise of power in accordance with the rule of law," and the "separation of powers and independence of the branches of government" are—among others—essential elements of democracy. The absence of those elements makes democracy non-existent and gives rise to authoritarianism and dictatorship, where the scientific verification of cases that represent the violation or disappearance of democratic rights is important.

Within this framework, the Interamerican Institute for Democracy and the Inter-American Bar Association—as think tanks whose objectives include the defense of human rights, fundamental freedoms, the rule of law, democracy, and justice—have set out to compile "case studies" of court rulings whose content and decisions may violate human rights. These are not political analyses; rather, they are strictly academic studies of legal cases that examine, with scientific rigor, specific prosecutions and judicial decisions in light of the rights enshrined in the Universal Declaration of Human Rights, which is in turn reflected in the constitutional texts of the states at issue.

This first study concerns judicial rulings that violate human rights in Ecuador. Similar studies are underway on judicial decisions in Cuba, Venezuela, Bolivia, and Nicaragua. It is an effort to bring within the field of scientific evidence what until now has been limited to political debate, press coverage, and victims' complaints.

It is an effort to shed light on some of the victims of judges who, rather than protecting their human rights, have instead violated them. These are studies performed by independent professionals who, with their legal expertise, seek to help restore of the rule of law and judicial independence in countries that—like Ecuador—have turned justice into a systematic mechanism for violating human rights.

Knowledge of these cases and dissemination of the expert presented in these studies are an effective contribution to the defense of human rights, singling out those governments that, outside the bounds of democracy, manipulate justice for the purpose of political pressure or repression.

September 2016
Armando Valladares
Human Rights Committee
Interamerican Institute for Democracy

PRESENTATIONS: JUDICIALIZED REPRESSION IN ECUADOR

Without checks and balances, democracy neither functions nor endures. This is the lesson of history. Absent effective checks on executive power, democracy tends to descend into authoritarianism, and authoritarianism to harden into dictatorship.

Regrettably, some governments of the left in our hemisphere tend to pursue their ends – whether good (benefiting the poor) or bad (consolidating a caudillo) – at the cost of checks and balances that are especially important for democracy. Among those essential institutions most under attack are independent judiciaries, free and critical media, political dissidents and social movements.

President Rafael Correa of Ecuador – presumably committed to the welfare of his people – appears not to appreciate the indispensable role of checks and balances. To be sure, Ecuador enjoys important elements of democracy. For example, the US State Department Country Report on Human Rights for 2015 acknowledges that President Correa won reelection in 2013 in voting that was "generally free and fair." The report also recognizes that civilian authorities in Ecuador maintain effective control over the security forces.

Nonetheless, according to the report, "The main human rights abuses were lack of independence in the judicial sector; [and] restrictions on freedom of speech, press, assembly, and association" (in addition to corruption). The report specifies that judges "reached decisions based on media influence or political and economic

9

pressures in cases where the government expressed interest." It adds that, according to human rights lawyers, "the government also ordered judges to deny all 'protection action' legal motions that argued that the government had violated an individual's constitutional rights to free movement, due process, and equal treatment before the law."

These State Department assessments would doubtless be rejected by President Correa as Yankee imperialism, unworthy of credibility. But similar conclusions can be found in the reports of independent organizations and experts. A serious and credible example is the 2014 report, *Independencia judicial en la reforma de la justicia ecuatoriana*, sponsored by three prestigious civil society organizations: the Due Process of Law Foundation, based in Washington; DeJusticia, of Colombia; and the Instituto de Defensa Legal, of Peru. The report's author is Luis Pasara of Peru, a recognized expert and academic in matters of judicial independence. According to the three organizations, the evidence in his report "clearly demonstrates the deplorable use of the judicial system, specifically the criminal justice system, as an instrument at the service of government interests, in contravention of respect for judicial independence, and with high costs for democratic institutionality."

The Pasara report analyzes twelve cases of social or political importance in Ecuador, prosecuted after the judicial reform of 2011, as well as some 42 resolutions of the Council on the Judiciary issued in other cases during the same period. The author concludes that there "currently exists in Ecuador a political utilization of justice that seriously compromises judicial independence."

Similar conclusions are evidenced in the current report, *El uso del poder judicial para vulnerar los derechos humanos en el Ecuador* (2016) (*The use of the judiciary to violate human rights in Ecuador*), sponsored by the Interamerican Institute for Democracy and the Interamerican Federation of Lawyers. The report presents six case studies. According to the sponsoring organizations, these criminal proceedings were used by Ecuadoran authorities to "harass, intimidate, persecute, silence and prosecute students, indigenous persons, people who denounce corruption, business owners and political dissidents."

The six cases are summarized by their respective authors in the text of the report. Accordingly, I do not here pretend to summarize either the cases or all the violations of due process. It suffices simply to highlight some of the violations, in order to illustrate the excesses that appear to have been committed.

The Cases

In the case of the **Ten of Luluncoto,** ten young people were arrested during a meeting. According to them, the meeting was for the purpose of planning their participation in an indigenous march for Water, Life, and Dignity of Peoples. The prosecutors alleged a different motive: an attempt to organize terrorism. However, when the arrests took place, the prosecutors had not identified any specific criminal charge. Worse, in spite of the apparent absence of individualized evidence against the majority of the youths, they were all ordered into pretrial detention: one for three months, seven for nine months, and two for a year. The criminal proceedings lasted four years. In the end the National Court of Justice dismissed the charges with prejudice. If there were truly evidence that the youths participated in terrorism, is this result credible?

The case of **Sebastian Cevallos** involves a political dissident who, in a series of tweets, disclosed a list of relatives of a high public official who held government jobs. One tweet stated that Paula Rodas, a niece of the high public official, held her government job, "effectively, [her uncle] is the minister of employment of his family."

The implication was that she had gained her position thanks to her uncle's political support. But she responded that, in fact, she won a merit-based competition to earn her position. She filed a criminal complaint against the tweeter for the crime of making "expressions in discredit or dishonor against another." The tweeter was convicted, fined, and sentenced to 15 days in prison.

Nonetheless, once the sentence was confirmed, Ms. Rodas pardoned the tweeter and asked that the case be dropped. In order to avoid prison, the tweeter accepted the arrangement. The court approved it.

Both the proceeding and the precedent are troubling. It would have been possible to respond to the tweeter with a public denial, a demand for retraction or clarification, or even a civil suit for defamation. To criminally prosecute for a tweet that implies something negative but mistaken about a public official is disproportionate and threatening to free expression.

For example, Principle 11 of the *Declaration of Principles on Freedom of Expression*, approved by the Inter-American Commission on Human Rights, declares that, "

In this case a different law was used to penalize the criticism, but free expression was equally violated. The effect of such criminalization can be to intimidate those who dare to criticize public officials on the internet.

Another political dissident, *Francisco Daniel Endara Daza*, was sentenced to 18 months in prison for the crime of "paralyzing public services." In the absence of evidence of his direct participation in acts damaging the property of Ecuador TV on 10 September 2010, when there was a sort of police uprising against President Correa, Mr. Endara was convicted for "applauding" the demonstrators. The unacceptability of both his conviction and his punishment speaks for itself.

In another case of "paralyzing public services," the case of the *29 of Saraguro*, an indigenous group blocked the Panamerican Highway. Two of the demonstrators were sentenced to four years in prison. The disproportionality of their sentence is obvious.

The case of the seizure of the television media, *TC Television and Gamavision*, was justified on the basis of criminal cases brought against the effective owners of the media enterprises. At first, both the Prosecutor General and the Supreme Court found no basis to prosecute the owners. In response, President Correa, as well as various legislators of his party, publicly declared their disagreement and demanded the dismissal and sanctioning of the judges. The new judges, amenable to Correa's political forces, sentenced the owners to eight years in prison.

Upon examining the case, the Human Rights Committee of the United Nations condemned the seizure of the television properties as a violation of due process. However, despite the dissenting vote of Committee member Yuval Sheny, the majority did not consider the public statements about the case by President Correa to

13

constitute undue interference with the independence of judiciary. With all respect, I believe that Dr. Sheny, and not the majority, was correct. In Ecuador, when President Correa speaks, judges listen.

This reality was demonstrated with equal clarity in the sixth case, that of the *students of Central Technical High School*. Twelve students of the school were among 600 students demonstrating against the change of name of the school proposed by the Ministry of Education. The prosecutor in the case decided not to bring charges against the 12 students, for lack of sufficient evidence of their guilt. The judge agreed.

Two days later, President Correa criticized the decisions of the prosecutor and judge. He insisted that they feared to rule against the students in the face of media pressure. The events were not a simple social protest, he declared, but criminal acts. As long as he remained President he would not permit this kind of behavior by "boys acting out of place" ("muchachos desubicados").

Two days later, the Provincial Prosecutor revoked the decision not to prosecute and took the 12 students to trial. They were then convicted of rebellion.

In other words, by his public declarations in this and other cases of political interest, President Correa has effectively converted himself into the highest court of appeal in Ecuador.

A Note of Clarification

In order to analyze violations of due process, it is neither necessary nor relevant to determine the innocence or guilt of the persons being prosecuted. For example, the seizure of the television media TC Television and Gamavision was justified on the basis of criminal cases brought against the owners. There are accusations of corruption against the owners, concerning which I am not sufficiently informed to opine. Nonetheless, for purposes of this report, this does not matter: even on the assumption of their guilt – bearing in mind the presumption of innocence – there is no justification for violating their right to a fair trial.

Two Caveats

The studies in the current report appear to demonstrate violations of judicial independence as well as the politicized use of criminal trials. However, two *caveats* should be mentioned. The first is that the authors of some of the studies are the defense lawyers for the accused. This fact diminishes the appearance, and possibly the reality, of the objectivity of the studies. Nonetheless, even with this limitation, the reports present evidence which is *prima facie* convincing of irregularities in the trials (as described above). In addition, these studies should be evaluated in the context of other reports, by diverse organizations, which also criticize the lack of judicial independence in cases of interest to the government in Ecuador.

The second *caveat* is the absence in the report of a response from the State. In the judgment of this writer, it is preferable that reports on violations of human rights in a country, if feasible, invite the observations of the State and include them, or at least a summary, in the report.

In spite of these *caveats*, the current report is a valuable contribution to public debate about the politicization of justice in Ecuador.

Conclusion

The six cases in the report should be cause for concern by everyone committed to judicial independence and justice free of politics in Ecuador. One hopes that the report may be read, pondered and debated in Quito.

Douglass Cassel
September 2016
University of Notre Dame

FOREWORD: INTER-AMERICAN BAR ASSOCIATION

This book compiles six case studies on human rights violations in Ecuador whose common denominator is—as the book's title suggests—*judicial decisions that infringe human rights in Ecuador.*

At first sight, this topic seems contradictory in its own terms. This is because, traditionally, in Latin America victims suffered human rights abuses from government agencies such as the police or military forces, but not directly from the judiciary. The victims sometimes sought relief from the courts of justice, but for politically motivated human rights abuses many countries denied the victims access to the courts. These victims eventually submitted their complaints to international human rights institutions.

However, a "new generation" of human rights violations has evolved, which is what the title of this book conveys. These new human rights violations take place primarily within the States' judicial apparatus. The governments or authorities wishing to commit harm against a person formulate "any" kind of legal action, with the willing involvement of prosecutors and judges, to initiate a judicial proceeding. They may initiate criminal, administrative, or even civil proceedings. Afterwards, the inefficiency and lack of independence of some of the Latin American judicial structures destroys the live and dignity of these victims. The courts of justice have become the new accomplices of ruthless rulers and corrupt public authorities. Ecuador confirms this trend, even after the 2011-2013 judicial reform, which initially attempted at modernizing Ecuador's judicial function and at increasing the system's independence.[1] International human rights bodies are starting to take notice of this phenomenon, although often this recognition is only partial and focused on the persecution of particularly vulnerable groups, such as human rights defenders[2] and journalists.[3] The procedural abuses committed by the judiciary can take place by way of lack of a balanced and reasoned evaluation of the evidence, lack of relevant and independent criminal investigation, the extension *ad aeternum* of judicial proceedings, the forced removal of judges who are not biased against the victim, the imposition of "provisional measures" that freeze all the victims' assets during the judicial

---

1. See also L. PASARA, *Independencia judicial en la reforma de la justicia ecuatoriana*, DPLF, Washington, D.C., 2014, who explained, when referring to the Judiciary Council's disciplinary powers, that "it aimed at the judges coming in line with the government's policies" (*id.*, p. 7). See on this also S. FARITH, "(No) independencia judicial", *El Comercio*, 4 August 2014, available online at http://www.elcomercio.com/opinion/no-independencia-judicial-1.html. For a well-researched critique of the outcomes of the Ecuadorian judicial reform from 2011-2013, see E. GUERRERO SALGADO, "Reforma judicial como prueba de la democracia delegativa en Ecuador: análisis institucional y comportamiento de la función ejecutiva", *Revista de Estudios Jurídicos*, Quito – Ecuador, No. 4 (December 2015), 68-81, especially pp. 75-78.
2. See, for instance, the latest report by the Inter-American Human Rights Commission, *Criminalization of the Work of Human Rights Defenders*, OEA/Ser.L/V/II.Doc. 49/15, paras. 29-31, where the Commission recognized the close link between judicial persecution of human rights defenders and the attack against democracy. Although human rights defenders contribute substantially to preserving the democratic institutions, the problem is broader tan only human rights defenders. The problem includes any lawyer that defends individuals who are persecuted by the State.
3. See the report by the Inter-American Human Rights Commission, Office of the Special Rapporteur on Freedom of Expression, *Freedom of Expression and the Internet*, OEA/Ser.L/V/II. CIDH/RELE/INF 11/13, of 31 December, 2013, where the authors reiterate the need for a pluralistic vision of internet freedom and access (*id.*, paras. 18-19).

investigation and thus deprive them of their resources to pay for effective legal counsel, and many other measures. This new type of human rights violation is more sophisticated than the blunt measures taken by previous generations of autocratic leaders, who had their victims kidnapped, tortured, and summarily executed. The result, however, is similar: people who suffer from oppressive justice systems are excluded from society and political life. They will not be able to take part in any democratic political process. In addition, in countries like Ecuador, the weak parliamentary structures and extensive powers of the Presidency have allowed the adoption of laws that create quasi-judicial procedures which operate parallel to the ordinary judiciary. These serve to oppress human rights. For example, the Ecuadorian 2013 Organic Law on Communications[4] created such procedures for alleged libel and slander cases against public authorities, which so far have caused substantial harm to the freedom of expression in that country.

Today, most victims of human rights violations have the right to access international human rights mechanisms. If we focus on Ecuador, victims may chose between a wide array of human rights bodies, primarily those of the United Nations and the Inter-American Human Rights System.

In the United Nations, victims can bring individual complaints to the Human Rights Committee for violations of all classic civil and political rights, as outlined in the International Covenant on Civil and Political Rights.[5]

---

4. Published in *Registro Oficial, Tercer Suplemento*, Año I, No. 22, of 25 June 2013.

5. Adopted on 16 December 1966, *UNTS*, vol. 999, p. 171. Ecuador acceded in 1969. Ecuador also acceded in 1969 to the Covenant's Optional Protocol that provides for an individual complaints procedure.

Alternatively, they can submit their claims to the Committees against Torture,[6] on Enforced Disappearance,[7] on the Elimination of All Forms of Discrimination against Women,[8] on the Elimination of All Forms of Racial Discrimination,[9] on Economic, Social and Cultural Rights,[10] and on the Rights of Persons with Disabilities.[11]

Regarding the Inter-American Human Rights System, the victims of human rights violations in Ecuador may present their cases to the Inter-American Human Rights Commission.[12] Regardless of the mechanism the victim choses, the final resolution will be binding upon the State as an emanation of the treaty's binding force, although it is not an international judgment with immediate enforceability.

---

6. This Committee was established under to the Convention Against Torture and Other Cruel, Inhuman or Degrading Treatment or Punishment, 10 December 1984, *UNTS*, vol. 1465, p. 85. Ecuador acceded in 1988.

7. This Committee was established under the International Convention for the Protection of All Persons from Enforced Disappearance, 20 December 2006, GA resolution 61/177, of 12 January 2007. Ecuador acceded in 2009.

8. This Committee was established under the Convention on the Elimination of All Forms of Discrimination Against Women, 18 December 1979, *UNTS*, vol. 1249, p. 13. Ecuador acceded in 1981.

9. This Committee was established under the International Convention on the Elimination of All Forms of Racial Discrimination, 21 December 1965, *UNTS*, vol. 660, p. 195. Ecuador acceded in 1966.

10. This Committee was established under the International Covenant on Economic, Social and Cultural Rights, 16 December 1966, *UNTS*, vol. 993, p. 3. Ecuador acceded in 1969.

11. This Committee was established under the Convention on the Rights of Persons with Disabilities, General Assembly resolution 61/106, of 24 January 2007. Ecuador acceded in 2008.

12. Pursuant to the American Convention on Human Rights, adopted at the Inter-American Specialized Conference on Human Rights, San José, Costa Rica, 22 November 1969. Ecuador ratified this treaty in 1977. On the procedure before the Inter-American Human Rights Commission, see B. Arp, *Las peticiones individuales ante la Comisión Interamericana de Derechos Humanos. Una guía práctica*, Ed. Porrúa, Mexico, 2014, in particular pp. 223-304.

Only the judgments of the Inter-American Human Rights Court have the legal force of an international judgment.

Regardless of the technicalities of each of these complaint mechanisms, their greatest contribution lies in that they declare the international responsibility of the State, as well as the consequences of this responsibility. These consequences include the obligation to repair the damages caused by the human rights violation, through payment of compensation or other measures. For instance, the bodies of the Inter-American Human Rights System have ordered States to reinstate judges that have been dismissed as reprisals, and to release from prison persons unjustly detained. In practice, the resolutions on individual human rights cases are a very important public recognition of the wrong committed by the affected State against the victim and thus rehabilitate — at least partially — the victim's dignity.

Regardless of the legal and symbolic importance of these mechanisms, they are not always an efficient solution to the problems faced in the member States. Four characteristics may be identified that hinder the mechanisms' efficiency in an ideal scenario. First, these international human rights mechanisms are composed of individuals who have been nominated by the mechanisms' member States. These are the same States against which the mechanisms are handling the human rights cases. Second, international NGOs have increasingly permeated the human rights mechanisms, pursuing often their own agendas beyond the strict boundaries of an independent, international, human rights enforcement mechanism. Third, the States finance these mechanisms, and hence they influence the mechanisms' efficiency through the increase or reduction of funding. For instance, in Latin America, the reduction of the States' contributions to the budget of the Inter-American Human Rights System has contributed to reduce its efficiency.[13] Fourth, and last, the international human rights mechanisms depend on the voluntary and spontaneous compliance by the States with the mechanisms' resolutions on human rights cases. The States, however, often do not comply, or only comply partially, with these resolutions.[14]

The victims feel the consequences of these characteristics of the international human rights mechanisms whenever they address their complaints to them. These particularities also explain why the real change in the judicial systems of the Latin American countries must come from within the affected countries.

This book points towards the problems of the judicial system in Ecuador, and formulates solutions needed within Ecuador to remedy these shortcomings. I hope this book raises the awareness about the risks of the usurpation of the courts of justice by the governments, and I encourage the authors to continue the international denunciation of these judicially made human rights violations.

Dr. Björn Arp

Inter-American Bar Association

Washington, D.C., February, 2017

---

13. See the press release from the Inter-American Human Rights Commission, *Severe Financial Crisis of the IACHR Leads to Suspension of Hearings and Imminent Layoff of Nearly Half its Staff*, May 23, 2016, available online at http://www.oas.org/en/iachr/media_center/PReleases/2016/069.asp (last accessed on February 10, 2017).

14. For an overview of the compliance monitoring of judgments and resolutions on provisional measures, see Inter-American Court of Human Rights, *Annual Report 2015*, San José, Costa Rica, 2016, pp. 54-85.

I

TO PRISON FOR A TWEET: THE JUDICIARY AS A TOOL FOR SILENCING LEGITIMATE EXPRESSION IN ECUADOR

By Daniela Salazar Marin[15].

1. Executive Summary

This text studies the case of Sebastian Cevallos, a young Twitter user who was subjected to criminal prosecution after disseminating information about cases of alleged nepotism in President Rafael Correa's government. Although the information and opinions he disseminated constituted speech protected by the right to freedom of expression that, as such, deserves broad currency in a democratic society, the judge sentenced Cevallos to prison. The opening criminal proceedings alone had a chilling effect on others who rely on social media as the only space left in Ecuadorian society to freely express opinions and ideas that challenge the actions and policies of the current administration. The case illustrates how the judiciary has become an important actor in silencing critics in Ecuador, even online.

2. Introduction

Analyzing a decision that shows how human rights are violated by the judiciary in Ecuador is not difficult. What is truly hard is to choose—among so many rulings—which

---

15. Abogada (LL.B.), Universidad San Francisco de Quito. LL.M., Columbia University. Faculty Member, Universidad San Francisco de Quito College of Jurisprudence. Former Human Rights Specialist, Inter-American Commission on Human Rights.

one best demonstrates how justice is used in our country to silence critical voices. Some cases involving the criminalization of protest in Ecuador have already had international impact. That is why I opted to analyze a case that has not enjoyed as much visibility, but in my opinion speaks for itself about the state of justice in Ecuador.

It relates to the criminal proceedings[16] opened against Rodrigo Sebastian Cevallos Vivar for publishing tweets that denounced alleged nepotism in President Rafael Correa's government. The ruling in the case not only confers greater value to a public official's reputational rights over Sebastian Cevallos' right to freely express himself and that of his followers to receive the information and opinions that Sebastian published through his Twitter account—it also sends a strong message to Ecuadorian society: a tweet can send you to prison if the government does not like what you publish.

This article's purpose is to analyze the judicial decision and its ill motives, with the aim of showing how, given the impossibility of regulating the Internet, the government has manipulated justice to generate an inhibitory effect on the right to seek, receive, express, and disseminate online information and ideas that are uncomfortable for the current administration.

3. Context and Facts of the Case

Since the Organic Communications Law took effect in Ecuador,[17] the traditional media has found itself subject to a

---

2. Paula Francisca Rodas Espinoza v. Rodrigo Sebastian Cevallos Vivar, *Proceso* [Case] No. 01283-2015-04771, Judicial Crim. Unit of Cuenca (Cayetano Alfredo Serrano Rodriguez, J.).

17. *Ley Organica de Comunicacion* [Organic Communications Law], *Registro Oficial* [Official Register] [R.O.] No 22 (June 25, 2013) (Ecuador).

system of control incompatible with the right to freedom of expression. The censorship imposed by the Superintendence of Communication and Information through its constant sanctions on the media, compounded by the self-censorship of the media itself — which as a matter of survival would rather abstain from reporting on matters that might inconvenience the government — has led to much of the discussion on matters of public interest migrating onto the Internet. Digital media and social networks have developed into an essential space for speaking out against corruption and human rights violations in Ecuador. Yet while it may be that the opinions and information that we spread through the Internet have eluded restraint by the Superintendence of Communication, the government's zeal to censor any expression critical of the regime has led has led it to wield the criminal laws to punish that expression.

Rodrigo Sebastian Cevallos Vivar is a young political leader. He serves as deputy director of the *Unidad Popular* leftist movement, and in July 2015, he published a series of tweets exposing that roughly twenty relatives of the then-minister of labor, Carlos Marx Carrasco, also held public appointments. Through his account, @sebastcevallos, he reported, among other things, that Marx Carrasco's daughters, Gabriela and Silvia Carrasco, held political positions, respectively, as ministerial adviser and managing director at a government-owned company that manages hydroelectric projects.

As part of his reporting on potential nepotism by the former labor minister, he wrote a tweet stating, "Paula Rodas, Carlos Marx Carrasco's niece, is on the NICH-Regional 6, indeed, he is the minister of his family's labor."

That tweet—which does not contain any speech unprotected by the right to freedom of expression, such as hate speech or incitements to violence—was enough for a judge to convict him.

Sentenced to prison, notwithstanding the fact that architect Paula Rodas is actually a public servant who has worked for the National Institute of Cultural Heritage since July 2008, and only six years later won a contested, merits-based selection process for her post. And sentenced to prison, notwithstanding the fact that during the proceedings, it was proven that Carlos Marx Carrasco, ex-director of the Internal Revenue Service and former Minister of Labor, is in fact Paula Rodas's uncle by marriage.

At the hearing, the Twitter user relied on content of what he expressed in his tweet, because this was not a case of publishing false information. Breaking down the tweet into its basic elements makes clear that it consists of two true facts—the public office of the complainant and her kinship to Carlos Marx Carrasco—and an opinion, which, as such, cannot be subjected to a veracity test, let alone give rise to criminal penalties. Nevertheless, he was convicted.

4. The Criminal Prosecution Against Sebastian Cevallos

Sebastian's crime, in the words of the complainant's counsel, was:

> "[t]o publish the twitters and retwitters [sic] relaying to the masses that Paula Francisca Rodas Espinoza is Carlos Marx Carrasco's niece and was working in the

public sector, when in truth, Paula Francisca Rodas Espinoza, has been working since the year 2008, as emergency Decree Technician, in the National Institute of Cultural Patrimony, and works until the present date, having been a participant and winner of contested, merits-based selection process, without Carlos Marx Carrasco, her uncle by marriage, having had anything to do with it."[18]

Thus, according to the complainant, the only admissible truth is that her public position relates solely to her own merits, and that her uncle was not involved. A clarification through another Twitter account, perhaps even an official one, would have been enough to set the facts straight—if they had in fact been false. But to call into doubt what the Minister's niece considers an unquestionable truth was enough for her to demand that the tweet's author be charged with "the maximum penalty provided under Comprehensive Organic Criminal Code article 396(1)," which provides:

"Fourth class contraventions. A sanction of fifteen to thirty days imprisonment shall be imposed on [t]he person who, by any means, utters expressions of discredit or dishonor against another."[19]

The functionary, her lawyer, and—what is worse—the presiding judge forgot that we citizens have not only the right, but the obligation, to hold public administration

---

18. Case No. 01283-2015-04771 (errors in the original).
19. *Codigo Organico Integral Penal* [Comprehensive Organic Criminal Code] [COIP], R.O. Supp. No. 180 (Feb. 10, 2014).

accountable—which includes our right to be informed about the degrees of kinship connecting our public officials, just as much as the reasons why contracts and salaries are paid with public funds. Like it or not, they are subject to our scrutiny.

It is worth noting that the suit is not limited to that tweet, but further seeks to hold Cevallos liable for re-tweets of content from his account. According to the lawyer who represented Paula Rodas, a re-tweet "is nothing more than to respond with will and conscience and own act."[20] In the lawyer's opinion, "it is proved, not only that they are of [Cevallos'] authorship and writing and own act of the agent, the *twitts* and *retwitts* [sic]"[21]. Despite the attorney's evident ignorance about the workings of the Internet and the Twitter social media platform, the judge was persuaded.

The defense sought to explain to the judge that this would mean also trying Sebastian over tweets that made no reference to the niece in question, as well as for the opinions of third parties over whom he had no control. Despite the defense's efforts, the judge weighed among the evidence used to condemn Cevallos not only his tweets, but also 11 retweets.

The niece's lawyer's exploitation of her female gender status to establish her reputational harm deserves further comment. Proceeding as if men and women had unequal or different reputational rights, the complainant argued that the tweet should be punishable because it "tarnishes the reputation of a woman who is a gestational state, of a Cuencan lady, and of a professional who has known

20. Case No. 01283-2015-04771.
21. Case No. 01283-2015-04771 (errors in the original).

how to work and earn things by her own efforts." Such dishonor was undeserved, he continued, by "anyone who comes from a proper home, such as the client whose reputation [he] defended, who did not earn an Architecture degree, by gift or raffle, but has achieved it with her tenacious effort, who has gotten her family ahead and led a dignified life [...]." To sum up, her lawyer requested "that justice be done in a lady's favor, who did not deserve such a dishonor." The level of legal argumentation is so poor, that it relieves me of any obligation to analyze it.

At the hearing, Cevalles clearly explained that Paula Rodas is a public official and, as such, is subject to public scrutiny. His defense team further brilliantly explicated the content and scope of the right to freedom of expression and its development across constitutional and inter-American jurisprudence.

Relying on inter-American standards — according to which the state's duty not to interfere with the right to access to information of all kinds extends to the circulation of information, ideas, and expressions that may or may not enjoy the personal blessing of those who represent state authority at a given moment[22] — the defense argued that:

> "freedom of expression must be ensured not with respect to the dissemination of ideas, information received favorably, considered harmless or neutral, but with respect to those that offend, shock, disturb, result unpleasant to or disturb the State, or any sector of the

22. Olmedos Bustos v. Chile ("The Last Temptation of Christ"), Merits, Reparations, and Costs, Inter-Am. Ct. H.R. (Ser. C) No. 73 ¶ 61(c) (Feb. 5, 2001).

population[;] that is what is required by pluralism, tolerance and the spirit of openness, without which there is no democratic society."[23]

Cevallos's defense also impeccably explained the doctrine of protected speech, according to which certain expressions (which are labeled "speech," regardless of their format) receive special protection under the right to freedom of expression—among them discourse on political and public-interest matters. According to the Inter-American Court of Human Rights:

"The expression of statements, information and opinions regarding matters of public interest, the State and its institutions enjoy greater protection under the American Convention on Human Rights. This means that the State must refrain more rigorously from placing limitations on these forms of expression, and that State entities and officials, as well as those who aspire to hold government positions, must have a higher threshold of tolerance in the face of criticism because of the public nature of their duties."[24]

With respect to that, Cevallos' defense argued that:

---

23. Case No. 01283-2015-04771.
24. Inter-Am. Comm'n on Human Rights, Office of the Special Rapporteur for Freedom of Expression, Inter American Legal Framework Regarding the Right to Access to Information, OEA Ser.L/V/II CIDH/RELE/INF. 2/09, at ¶ 35 (Dec. 30, 2009) (citing Palamara Iribarne v. Chile, Merits, Reparations, and Costs, Inter-Am. Ct. H.R. (Ser. C) No. 135, ¶ 83 (Nov. 22, 2005)); Herrera Ulloa v. Costa Rica, Preliminary Objections, Merits, Reparations, and Costs, Inter-Am. Ct. H.R. (Ser. C) No. 107, ¶ 125-29 (July 2, 2004); *id.* at ¶ 101(2)(c).

"Public officials and those who aspire to be them in a democratic society, enjoy a different threshold of protection that exposes them to greater scrutiny and criticism from the public, which is justified by its general-interest nature. Because expressions and information pertaining to public officials, individuals voluntarily involved in public affairs, and candidates for public office enjoy a greater degree of protection, the State should refrain in greater measure from imposing limitations on these forms, in this case, of speech...."[25]

The defense clearly explained that not only did the Twitter user have the right to publicly scrutinize this public official, but the community at large has the right to know whether various public officials are related to a minister, and to draw their own conclusions. The argument is grounded in established inter-American jurisprudence, which casts freedom of expression as a norm with two dimensions: an individual dimension, which is the right of each person to express his or her own thoughts, ideas, and information; and a collective or social dimension, which consists of society's right to seek and receive any information; to know others' thoughts, ideas, and information; and to be well-informed[26].

Despite this categorical defense, the judge showed a very limited capacity for understanding. Faced with the

---

25. Case No. 01283-2015-04771.
26. Kimel v. Argentina, Merits, Reparations, and Costs, Inter-Am. Ct. H.R. (Ser. C)No. 177 ¶ 53 (May 2, 2008); Claude Reyes v. Chile, Merits, Reparations, and Costs, Inter-Am. Ct. of H.R. (Ser. C) No. 151 ¶ 75 (Sept. 19, 2006); Herrera Ulloa, *supra* note 10, at ¶ 108; Ivcher Bronstein v. Peru, Merits, Reparations, and Costs, Inter-Am. Ct. H.R. (Ser. C) No. 74, ¶ 146 (Feb. 6, 2001); Canese v. Paraguay, Merits, Reparations, and Costs, (Ser. C) No. 111, ¶ 77 (Aug. 31, 2004).

doctrine of protected speech, the judge held that "Cevallos Vivar, has not, in any of the forms expressed through his twitter account, made any manifestations of the 'speech' type."[27] The judge, called to resolve a conflict between the reputational and speech rights at stake, evidently failed to understand the difference between the two. He further held that the "right to freedom of expression, in this judge's opinion, is curtailed because it disturbs the honor and dignity of Paula Rodas when it is stated that she has entered the public sector thanks to her uncle by marriage Carlos Marx Carrasco"[28].

The judgment entered by Judge Cayetano Alfredo Serrano Rodriguez on December 11, 2015, held that:

> "In accordance with the rules of Article 455 of the Comprehensive Code of Criminal Procedure, with the evidence presented, it has been possible to determine the materiality of the infraction, as well, as the culpability of the accused and its causal link. Materiality of the infraction from the print-outs from the twitter network, certified by Dr. Homero Moscoso Jaramillo, Notary Eighth of the Cuenca Quarter. [C]ulpability, inasmuch as Rodrigo Sebastian Cevallos Vivar, has recognized, in his testimony, free, voluntary and without oath, that with respect to carrying out the different twitters, does so based on the information obtained for the national interest, and in response to the social, economic and political problems faced by the country, and for the fact of denouncing acts of corruption by government officials, using the @sebastcevallos twitter network. [T]

---

27. Case No. 01283-2015-04771.
28. *Id.*

herefore, the behavior of Rodrigo Sebastian Cevallos Vivar behavior, falls within the illegal, culpable, and criminally defined conduct under Article 396, subsection 1, [i]n the manner provided in Articles 25, 29 and 34 of the Comprehensive Organic Criminal Code - For the foregoing reasons, this Authority ADMINISTERING JUSTICE IN THE NAME OF THE SOVEREIGN PEOPLE OF ECUADOR, BY AUTHORITY OF THE CONSTITUTION AND THE LAWS OF THE REPUBLIC," declares the guilt of the citizen: RODRIGO SEBASTIAN CEVALLOS VIVAR ... to be the perpetrator and responsible person for the criminal conduct, enacted in Numeral 1, Article 396, of the Comprehensive Organic Criminal Code, this is, that through his twitter network has made known to society, that Paula Francisca Rodas Espinoza, has joined the National Institute of Cultural Heritage, thanks to the favors of her uncle by marriage, then-Labor Minister Carlos Marx Carrasco, when in reality and in documented manner Paula Rodas has proven to have been admitted after wining a contested, merits-based selection process, for which, he is required to serve a 15-day prison term, to be served at the Center for Regional Social Rehabilitation Sierra Centro Sur-Turi, of this City of Cuenca, for which the constitutional warrant will be issued to legalize his imprisonment, likewise, as provided in Subsection 1, of Article 70 of the Comprehensive Criminal Code, a fine of twenty-five percent (25%) of a Unified Basic Salary of the General Worker [minimum wage] shall be imposed."[29]

---

29. *Id.*

Such is how Rodrigo Sebastian Cevallos Vivar was sentenced to fifteen days in prison based on tweets that any of us could have written, had we possessed information about roughly twenty public officials who are somehow relatives of the Minister of Labor. Questioning why so many officials are related to a Minister is absolutely legitimate, and society has the right to know this information — which as it happens, is public — as much as those affected have the right to correct the record if the information false. But there was nothing to rectify here — what mattered was to apply the punitive power of the state to punish someone who dared to question why so many of a minister's relatives hold public office.

Cevallos' defense team appealed the decision. On April 1, 2016, however, the Criminal Chamber of the Criminal Court of Justice of Azuay affirmed the conviction.[30] The relative leniency of the sentence — 15 days in prison and a small fine — does not make any less terrifying the state's use of criminal laws — the most punitive tool at its disposal — to penalize speech that is legitimate and protected by the fundamental right to freedom of expression. The judgment would have been an international scandal if not for what happened next.

As if the conviction itself did not clearly betray the state's abusive manipulation of the criminal laws to silence opponents, after the conviction had been affirmed on appeal but before it was executed, Paula Francisca Rodas Espinoza filed a motion pardoning Sebastian Cevallos, requesting that a criminal determination be entered

---

30. Special Judgment, Case No. 01283201504771, Paula Francisca Rodas Espinoza v. Rodrigo Sebastian Cevallos Vivar, Provincial Court of Azuay, Criminal Chamber.

in his favor, and expressly withdrawing from the criminal suit initiated against the Twitter user. [31]

As might be expected, the opportunity to avoid deprivation of his freedom gave the young Sebastian Cevallos much relief, and he had little choice but to go along with the complainant's "pardon" of a "crime" that actually wasn't. The Court accepted the petition for pardon on April 7, 2016, and ordered dismissal of the action against Cevallos. Having resolved the suit through that procedural mechanism, however, now prevents Sebastian Cevallos from turning to international forums to assert his right to freedom of expression and our collective right of access to information.

5. Conclusions

While this case has since been resolved with a "pardon," the mere opening of criminal proceedings has an inhibitory effect on other citizen's exercise of their free speech rights. Many will ask themselves whether sending a tweet that might discomfort a public official is worth losing their freedom, along with all of the other consequences that having a criminal history entails.

The case is particularly outrageous because, as the Inter-American Court of Human Rights has emphasized:

> "The operation of democracy demands the greatest possible degree of public debate on the functioning of

---

31. In Ecuador, this procedure is provided for under the Comprehensive Organic Criminal Code, which states: "Extinguishment of the exercise of criminal action.- The exercise of the criminal action will be extinguished by [...] [f]ree or voluntary resignation or resignation of the victim, withdrawal or transaction, in the crimes that proceed the private exercise of the action." COIP, *supra* note 5, at art. 416(2).

society and the State in all of their aspects, that is, on matters of public interest. In a democratic and pluralistic system, the acts and omissions of the State and of government officials must be subject to rigorous scrutiny, not only by the internal control authorities, but also by the press and by public opinion. The conduct of public affairs and issues of common interest must be controlled by society as a whole. The democratic control of government through public opinion encourages the transparency of State activities and the accountability of public officials for their actions, and is a mean of achieving the maximum degree of citizen participation. It follows that the adequate functioning of democracy requires the greatest possible circulation of reports, opinions and ideas on matters of public interest." [32]

Before using the criminal laws to restrict the right to freedom of expression, the judges who heard Sebastian Cevallos' case should have performed a test of strict proportionality. That is, they should have considered whether it really was necessary to apply criminal law, or whether there existed an alternative less burdensome on freedom of expression. Obviously, such an alternative existed—a tweet or even a press release disseminated via the multiple media outlets under the state's control would have been plenty to set the record straight—assuming it was even incorrect. As for any opinions derived from that information, those are not susceptible to any rectification

---

32. Inter American Legal Framework, *supra* note 10, at ¶ 33. Kimel, *supra* note 12 ¶¶ 57, 87; Claude Reyes, *supra* note 12 at ¶¶ 84, 86, and 87; Palmara Iribarne, *supra* note 5, at ¶ 83; Herrera Ulloa, *supra* note 5, at ¶ 127.

measures. The judges also were obligated to question whether the prison sentence, fines, and damages assessed as penalties in Sebastian's case were proportional to the damage alleged by the public official. Criminal law must be applied as a last resort and not as a means to send society a cautionary message. We are not dealing with speech that incites hatred or violence here, but rather speech entitled to special protection under the right to freedom of expression because it informs and opines on matters of public interest.

Although Paula Rodas' attorney failed to prove any actual harm to his client, he did manage to convince the judge that speech that results in discredit to another person "requires an exemplary penalty." What was sought through this criminal prosecution, then, is to send society a clear message: if you criticize the government's administration, you can go to prison; if you are going to make reference to a public official, you better clarify that he won a contested, merits-based selection process, has clean hands and a burning heart. Sending a cautionary message to generate societal fear is not a legitimate objective capable of justifying a penalty like that imposed on Sebastian.

If this decision is broadcast, its effect may not be what the government expects. The ruling is yet more proof of how the criminal laws are used to prosecute those who expose acts of corruption, while those who commit those acts remain unpunished. As the government wields criminal laws as a weapon to silence citizens who exercise their duty and right to participate in placing societal checks on public administration, we have social networks and digital media—the trenches from where we can access information and opinion on government abuse that the Prosecutor's Office refuses to investigate and that the traditional media fears to publish. That is my motivation for writing this piece. As the Inter-American Court of Human Rights has pointed out:

> "Democratic control exercised by society through public opinion encourages the transparency of State activities and promotes the accountability of public officials in public administration, for which there should be a reduced margin for any restriction on political debates or on debates on matters of public interest."[33]

---

33. Herrera Ulloa, *supra* note 5, at ¶ 127. *Also see* Ivcher Bronstein, *supra* note 12, at ¶ 155; Inter-Am. Comm'n on Human Rights, 1994 Annual Report, ch. 5 Report on the Compatibility of "Desacato" Laws with the American Convention on Human Rights, OEA/Ser.L./V/II.91 (Feb. 17, 1995).

II
TERRORISM FORGED IN A CONSTITUTIONAL STATE OF LAW: THE CASE OF "THE TEN OF LULUNCOTO"

By Dr. Jaime Vintimilla[34].

1. Executive Summary

On March 3, 2012, ten young people were arrested for alleged terrorism in the Luluncoto neighborhood south of Quito, Ecuador. The hearing to determine flagrancy was held on March 4. Upon criminal charges filed, a summons was issued for trial on the basis of Penal Code Article 160. On March 7, 2013, the Third Criminal Court convicted the ten youths of attempted terrorism, sentencing them to one year by written opinion dated May 15, 2013. On December 24, 2013, the Provincial Court of Pichincha rejected their appeal, upholding the judgment of the lower court. Moreover, on June 7, 2016, the National Court of Justice issued the judgment, where they applied the principle of favorability, in light of the fact that the subsequent law was more favorable.

2. Introduction.

The purpose of this case study titled "The Ten of Luluncoto" is to describe the serious human rights violations

---

34. Attorney and Doctor of Jurisprudence, Pontificia Universidad Catolica del Ecuador. Professor of Law, Universidad San Francisco de Quito. Graduate professor at Andean Simon Bolivar University (Quito) and Alcalá de Henares (Spain). Dr. Vintimilla has written more than 25 articles and books on constitutional and financial law, arbitration, mediation, history, genealogy, and indigenous justice.

carried out over the course of proceedings before various courts, focusing on the abuse of various protective measures, as well as the transgression of the criminal law principle of consistency through the distorted interpretation and application of the *iora novit curia* principle — all of which leads us down the dark path of legal theory of the Criminal Law of the Enemy.

3. Facts and Context

On November 11, three so-called "pamphlet bombs" linked to the *Combatientes Populares* group were set off in the cities of Quito, Guayaquil, and Cuenca. An operation named *Sol Rojo* (Red Sun) launched on March 3, 2012, with the search of an apartment located in the Luluncoto neighborhood, south of the capital city of Quito. Its purpose was to detain ten youths gathered there to decide on their participation in a march for water, dignity, and life and against mining operations, which the indigenous movement had announced would arrive in Quito on March 22, 2012.

4. The Process

The case of Ten of Luluncoto will go down in history — not as the case that was ultimately won, but as the one where ten innocent people were convicted to please and appease government agencies thirsting for "justice." Undoubtedly, the case will be remembered as an example of the grand failure of our judicial system.[35]

---

35. Torres, Juan Pablo, *Los 10 de Luluncoto*, GKILLCITY.COM (June 13, 2016), http://gkillcity.com/articulos/el-mirador-politico/los-10-luluncoto-ni-verdad-ni-justicia.

In any case, it is important to highlight some aspects of the administration of justice that pervade the history of our national state of affairs, namely:

a) Since the very founding of the republic, the Executive has interfered with the Judiciary in many ways.

b) The laws in effect are divorced from their application. Despite being rights-based (protective model), the Montecristi Constitution, unfortunately, has frequently been ignored and violated in practice, with it even being argued that because it provides so-called "hyper-guaranteeist" protections, the constitution must be reformed.

c) Despite changes in the normative paradigms of criminal law, an abusive reliance on preventive imprisonment has prevailed.[36]

d) Cases where political power is in play must be distinguished from those where it is absent. That distinction demarcates the degree of intervention by the Executive, which tends to be more accentuated in the former category.

In this context, the objective here is to study a case where players in the judicial system fail to defend certain constitutional rights of the accused, with the produced effect of intimidating students and professionals who oppose government policies. Unfortunately and paradoxically, these abuses take shape within the constitutional

---

36. VINTIMILLA, JAIME, DUE PROCESS OF LAW FOUNDATION, INDEPENDENCIA JUDICIAL INSUFICIENTE, PRISION PREVENTIVA DEFORMADA. LOS CASOS DE ARGENTINA, COLOMBIA, ECUADOR Y PERU [INSUFFICIENT JUDICIAL INDEPENDENCE, DEFORMED PRETRIAL DETENTION. THE CASES OF ARGENTINA, COLOMBIA, ECUADOR AND PERU], ECUADOR REPORT 1 (2013).

framework of a state where fundamental rights and rule of law supposedly prevail.

a) Facts

On the night of March 3, 2012, a group of 10 youths[37] gathered in an apartment located in Luluncoto, a neighborhood located in the southeast of Quito. All are students or professional graduates of state universities with trajectories as leaders.[38] According to Fadua Tapia's testimony

---

37. The youths' names and their ages are: Ana Cristina Campana Sandoval, 23; Fadua Elizabeth Tapia Jarrin, 18; Jesenia Abigail Heras Bermeo, 28; Cristhian Royce Gomez Romero, 25; Pablo Andres Castro Cangas, 24; Luis Santiago Gallegos Valarezo, 30; Victor Hugo Vinueza; Luis Marcelo Merchan Mosquera, 23; Victor Hector Estupinan Prado, 27; and Cesar Zambrano Farias, 18. *Las ideas detras de las rejas*, VANGUARDIA MAGAZINE (Nov. 26 – Dec. 2, 2012). Of the 10 persons investigated, seven are men and three are women. The men were held in the Pichincha provisional detention center and the two women in the "El Inca" prison. Fadua, because she was pregnant, was only detained for 12 hours at the Judicial Police and then confined to house arrest. According to Amnesty International, the ten were arrested without a warrant and were not found *in flagrante delicto* where they were congregated. All were charged pursuant to article 160 of the Criminal Code with the crime of committing terrorist acts and (with the exception of Tapia) detained until their trial and conviction. In short, they are accused of committing the crime of organized terrorism, defined under the Penal Code, as the persons allegedly responsible for the "pamphlet bombs" fired in Quito, Cuenca, and Guayaquil on November 17 and December 19, 2011, in protest of the visit of Colombian President Juan Manuel Santos. The prosecution also accuses them of planning new terrorist acts that were to take place at the National March promoted by CONAIE from March 8 to March 22, 2012.
38. Pablo Castro was president of the Ecuadorean Federation of High School Students and Luis Menchin was its provincial secretary in Guayas. Cristina Campana was presidential candidate for the Ecuadorean Federation of University Students and top student in her class. Victor Vinueza was vice president of the employee association of the Central University School of Philosophy. And so forth. *Panfletos son pruebas contra 'Los 10 de Luluncoto', acusados por el terrorismo*, EL COMERCIO (Dec. 5, 2012), *available at* http://www.elcomercio.com.ec/ seguridad/polemica-panfletos-acusacion-terrorismo_0_822517923.html.

on the day of the arrests, they had met "only to study the Constitution" and discuss the country's problems. But there are inevitably two accounts of the gathering—the version of the persons gathered and accused, and that of the police, the Ministry of the Interior, and the officers of the court.[39]

That night, the police's "Red Sun" operation linked the youths to the *Combatientes Populares* group that sought to destabilize the regime.[40] The jailings occurred at a momentous time, as the indigenous movement had announced its march for water, dignity, and life against mining operations, which would depart the Amazon on March 8, 2012, and would arrive Quito on March 22. Members of the police GIR (Intervention and Rescue Group) and ULCO (Anti-Organized Crime Unit) squads raided the site and accused the young people of planning the detonation of the so-called *bomba panfletaria* (pamphlet bomb).[41] It is worth noting that even before the arrests, the police had already launched an investigation into Royce Gomez's activities unbeknownst to the prosecution, a violation of article 76.4 of the Constitution that

---

39. AVILA, RAMIRO, PROGRAMA ANDINO DE DERECHOS HUMANOS, LOS DIEZ DE LULUNCOTO, ¿TERRORISTAS? 28 (2013), *available at* http://repositorio. uasb.edu.ec/bitstream/10644/ 4110/1/Avila%20Santamaria,%20 R-Los%20diez.pdf.
40. Police leads drew the investigation toward the *Grupo de Combatientes Populares* (Popular Combatants Group, or "GCP"), an organization that emerged in the late 1980s to early 1990s. Its Twitter page describes "[a]rmed struggle as the only way." On YouTube, it is described as a "military-political organization that conspires against capitalist society." *Todos hablan de revolucion*, REVISTA VISTAZO (May 2012).
41. A "pamphlet bomb" is a homemade explosive device that releases airborne leaflet propaganda.

would render invalid the arrest, search, and seizure of the group members and their property.[42]

At a hearing on July 25, 2012, before the Tenth Criminal Guarantees Court of Pichincha (the trial court in this case), prosecutor Jose Jaramillo accused the 10 of Luluncoto of alleged terrorism, because pages describing "phone calls (to alert about) explosives", "pamphlet bombs," and papers mentioning the *Grupo de Combatientes Populares* group had been found in the apartment during the arrest. "[I]mages, logos, and texts of an ideological type" similar to those that appeared after the bombs exploded were also found.[43] In other words, the trial summons lacked any basis on a bona fide investigation—let alone reliable evidence— given that the judge, among other discrepancies, explained that everything seized was "relevant" because there were documents "containing political slogans of the popular combatant's group." A trivial argument for setting trial under Criminal Code article 160, which carries a potential prison term of up to eight years.[44]

The Prosecutor's Office sustained its accusation based on 62 police accounts, according to Vladimir Andocilla, attorney for the youths' release. It is an unprecedented case. Police accounts were given weight over the youths' presumption of innocence and the submission of any of

---

42. AVILA, *supra* note 6, at 30.
43. Mobile phones, USB devices, cosmetics, mirrors, pennies, $20 bills, a bus ticket, a notebook with the phrase "building a corruption-free Ecuador," and other personal effects were logged among the evidence of a "potential terrorist offense" in an inventory signed by ULCO officers and incorrectly dated March 3, 2011. As described by Cristina Campana, a Sandinista handkerchief and her school's cheerleading uniform, both red, were evidence for the operation Red Sol police and prosecutors.
44. AVILA, *supra* note 5, at 30.

material evidence."[45] The result was that the prosecution linked the purported evidence collected from the apartment with the six explosions recorded between November 17 and 22, 2011.

Police further maintain that two writings were recovered from the three explosions that occurred on November 19 of that year. One of those contains messages opposing the visit to Ecuador of Colombian President Juan Manuel Santos and a drawing of him surrounded by skulls.

According to the prosecution, a similar image was found on the blog of Royce Gomez, who was also detained. One of the elements linking Gomez, a Guayaquil dentist and community organizer in the Guasmo neighborhood, to the explosions was a message on his Facebook page, where he expressed dissatisfaction with what he considered populist policies by Rafael Correa's administration. This was confirmed to *Vanguardia* magazine by the judicial police sergeant who created a fake profile on that social network to observe the young dentist's views.

The police also described the GCP's structure and its provincial and neighborhood commands, and explained the group's mission as the "seizure of state power through insurgency and armed struggle."

A report on this case by the human rights organizations CEDHU, INREDH, and *Clinica Ambiental* found human rights violations as well as psychological and social effects, including that:

---

45. *Las ideas tras las rejas, supra* note 3, at 15.

• Several human rights violations have been documented, particularly to the right to physical and psychological integrity during arrest and confinement, such as physical and verbal aggression, isolation, denial of information, and denial of health, among others.

• The bad conditions of prisons in Ecuador generally affect its population. Also, serious overcrowding issues breeds the proliferation of viral diseases without proper care. The members of the 10 of Luluncoto, rather than receiving medical care, were locked in a dungeon and denied medication. This amounts to cruel and degrading treatment, as well as denial of the right to health.

• There was also evidence of violations during arrest against a person deserving priority attention (here, due to pregnancy), who despite reporting her condition, was assaulted and denied medical attention for a prolonged period of time.

• The right to a proper defense was violated by changes of venue for hearings to define the accused's charges.

• Likewise, rights to privacy, reputation, image, and good name of the accused and their families were violated. Their faces were exposed to the mass media with statements that they were "terrorists," without regard for the presumption of innocence as a guiding principle.

When, at dawn on April 26, 2012, police squads in several cities stormed into the homes of relatives of the 10 detained youths searching for evidence, the physical and psychological integrity of the detainees and their families was violated in the search of their homes, as they were prevented from access to medication and from attending to children and the elderly present at the time.[46]

b. Criminal Proceedings Against the Ten of Luluncoto and Pretrial Custody

The procedural history of the case is as follows:

On March 4, 2012, the ten defendants were remanded into pretrial custody, because "most of them were not able to justify sufficient ties to the community"; thus, pretrial detention was not a last-resort measure.

On March 27, 2012, the Provincial Court denied the youths' appeal on the issue of pretrial detention, holding that freeing the accused "would alter the discovery of factual and legal proof required by due process" and holding it improper to substitute pretrial detention with other measures.[47]

The Third Criminal Court of Pichincha entered a verdict on May 15, 2013, finding the ten accused to be the perpetrators responsible for the crime of attempted terrorism. It sentenced each youth to a modified term of one year in a correctional facility and payment of a $1,767 fine.

On December 24, 2013, the specialized criminal chambers of the Pichincha Provincial Court of Justice dismissed the accused's appeals and pleas for annulment, upholding the Third Criminal Court's sentence.

---

46. *See generally* CEDHU ET AL., OCASO DE LA JUSTICIA. EL CASO SOL ROJO. INFORME PSICOSOCIAL Y DE DERECHOS HUMANOS, OPERATIVO SOL ROJO (2012), *available at* http://hdl.handle.net/10644/3989.

47. AVILA, *supra* note 6, at 33.

The condemned filed a cassation appeal before the criminal chambers of the National Court of Justice, an extraordinary appeal that was granted on January 21, 2014.

The specialized chamber for criminal, military criminal, police criminal, and transit matters of the National Court of Justice summoned hearing on the merits of the cassation appeal during the first week of March 2016, suspending the hearing to read its operative part on Tuesday, June 7, 2016.

On June 14, 2016, the Chamber issued the majority vote of two national judges, holding that "in this particular case, the principle of favorability has been applied" and therefore "the sentence is quashed as provided in [article] 72.2 of the Comprehensive Organic Criminal Code and "the personal and real interim measures on the convicted persons are lifted," to carried out by the lower courts.[48]

Finally, a dissenting vote was cast declaring the "constitutional nullity of the sentence issued by the criminal chambers of the Provincial Court of Justice," dated December 24, 2013, "because it was unreasonable".[49]

c) Irregular Aspects of the Proceedings at Trial, on Appeal, and on Extraordinary Appeal

48. The National Court of Justice panel majority applied the principle of favorability on the basis that the offense of which the Ten of Luluncoto were accused is not defined in the Comprehensive Organic Criminal Code, published in the Official Register Supplement Number 180 of February 10, 2014, which took effect on August 10 of that year. It boggles the mind, however, the amount of time spent by the judicial authorities to rule based on a statute that had been in effect since August 2014.
49. The rulings by the Criminal Court, the Provincial Court of Justice, and the National Court of Justice were communicated to the parties first, orally, and later by written decision.

Besides the obvious politicization of the handling of this case, a core aspect that needs to be highlighted is the lack of evidence. The finders of fact admitted evidence that was not presented according to constitutional, conventional, and legal rules, thus tainting their decisions and making them unconstitutional. Further, although the accused were released after a ruling was issued at the trial level because the length of pretrial detention exceeded the sentence issued, alternatives to custody were also imposed on them pending the outcome of appeal and cassation proceedings, to require their appearance before the competent forum.

Across the various stages of the proceedings, a series of postponements and delays prejudiced the accused. Among them, the most notable include two preliminary hearings dismissed for lack of prosecution; motions to quash, review, and modify interim measures were summarily thrown out; a hunger strike; a trial hearing postponed by the absence of one of the three judges of the Third Criminal Court[50]; and the trial hearing set for December 10, 2012, vacated because one of the judges abruptly fell ill.

Therefore, in a press release on January 16, 2013, the Ecumenical Commission for Human Rights (CEDHU) asked the prosecution and other judicial and civil servants to respect the human rights of the accused.[51] Among the CEDHU's requests, two stand out, namely:

---

50. Garcia, Ramiro, *En el ajedrez del gobierno, los jueces han terminado siendo peones*, PAISENVIVO (March 1, 2013), http://paisenvivo.com.ec/ramiro-garca-en-el-ajedrez-del-gobierno-los-jueces-han-terminado-siendo-peones/.

51. Upon learning of the irregularities in the process, human rights groups issued the report, OCASO DE LA JUSTICIA, *supra* note 13, which establishes violations of the human rights of the detainees and their

1. That Prosecutor Galo Chiriboga and the Judiciary Council monitor the actions of the judges and prosecutors in charge of the case because the repeated canceled hearings and postponements and excuses by judges could create a pattern and practice of denial of justice and human rights violations.

2. That minister Jose Serrano refrain from intervening in the case because his statements undermined the principle of judicial independence and the basic presumption that a person is innocent until proven otherwise.[52]

---

families in the raids on their homes. Noteworthy among the groups' observations is that the trial hearing scheduled for December 10 was suspended due to the absence of one the Third Court panel members, who excused himself last-minute on account of illness. The supposed illness lasted one day, and the next day he attended as normal. The detainees went on hunger strike starting December 7 in protest against the proceedings against them and the delay of the court system that, because it lacked conclusive evidence linking them to the crime of which they were accused, resorted to stalling the proceedings. The seven men were released on December 21, two days after the habeas corpus hearing, but Ana Cristina and Abigail were denied that remedy, notwithstanding that all 10 accused were party to the exact same criminal proceedings. That decision has been appealed to the National Court of Justice, which apparently has delayed in deciding it. Ana Cristina Campana and Abigail Heras remained on hunger strike, sustaining their protest for 30 days inside the El Inca women's prison in Quito; their health condition considerably worsened, and on the night of December 27, Abigail suffered fainting and muscular problems that impeded her mobility. Various requests were made for outside doctors to enter the Inca women's prison to monitor the health conditions of the detainees on an ongoing basis, but those requests have not been heard with the appropriate urgency. *See* Press Release, INREDH, Ministerio del Interior apela sentencia de habeas corpus a favor de los internos del Turi (Nov. 7, 2016) *available at* http://www.inredh.org/index.php?option=com_content&view=article&id=549.

52. *C.f.* Press Release, Ministerio del Interior del Ecuador, El gobierno previene ataques terroristas, no espera que ocurran para actuar (Dec. 12, 2012), *available at* http://www.ministeriointerior.gob.ec/el-gobierno-previene-atentados-terroristas-no-espera-que-ocurran-para-actu-

With respect to the constitutionality of the proceedings, the accused moved to vacate the proceedings (annulment) because, in carrying them out "the procedure provided by the law had been violated, influencing the decision in the case and tainting its validity, since March 3, 2012, when the police, acting on prosecutor's orders, carried out the first and unlawful search on the site where the now-prosecuted 10 youths were peacefully gathered."[53]

They also alleged that they were detained for seven hours without a hearing and that the arraignment hearing was later held on March 4, 2012, where, without legal grounds whatsoever, the prosecution was initiated and pretrial detention ordered by the Twenty-Second Criminal Guarantees Judge.[54]

They explained that during the preliminary hearing, the prosecutor did not name each of the defendants individually or describe particular acts in which they allegedly participated, as required by Criminal Procedure Code—issues that, taken together, constitute a violation of due process of law and of fundamental principles, guarantees, and constitutional rights such as legality, freedom, and presumption of innocence, among others.

---

ar. Ministry officials also publicly said on March 4, 2012, that the GCP members' goal was "to seize power by arms."

53. *Caso Los 10 de Luluncoto: Jueza niega pedido de nulidad de juicio*, Diario La Hora (Sept. 26, 2012), *available at* http://lahora.com.ec/index.php/noticias/show/1101399295/ 1/Caso_Los_10_de_ Luluncoto %3A_ Jueza_niega_pedido_de_nulidad_del_juicio.html #.WEfv8neZORs.

54. It is worth remembering that the prosecution requested pretrial detention because it considered that the 10 defendants failed to sufficiently establish their ties to the community, and also because they were accused of a crime punishable by imprisonment, and therefore would allegedly pose a danger to society if freed. The judge accepted those arguments and ordered pretrial detention, although greater violations occurred in the course of the arrest process.

Finally, it should be noted that on December 19, 2012, the first labor chambers of the Pichincha Provincial Court granted habeas corpus to the seven men involved in the case, but failed to extend the same relief to Abigail Heras or Cristina Campana, who continued in prison until the date of the conviction hearing.

As it relates to the conviction, it is important to note that the Third Criminal Court found the 10 youths accused by the Prosecutor's Office of acts in preparation against national security guilty of "attempted subversion," although they were arrested on March 3, 2012. Ramiro Garcia, one of the attorneys for the defense, said that the judges modified the charge at the last minute in order to convict them because the prosecution had failed to prove its accusations. He also claimed that the State used the sentence as a form of social pedagogy.[55]

What is true is that seven people were deprived of their liberty for ten months and two others for an entire year, where pretrial detention was used as an "anticipatory sentence" of sorts.

In the extraordinary appeal at the cassation level, the National Court of Justice's reluctance to reach the merits is evident. It was more comfortable, so to speak, resolving the appeal by application of the principle of favorability, without getting caught up in debating the guilt or innocence of the accused.

Separately, this also draws attention to the fact that, because during the review of the laws at issue there are no specific deadlines or time limits for the suspension

---

55. *10 de Luluncoto. El tribunal cambio la figura de la acusaction, la defense apelara*, DIARIO HOY (Feb. 27, 2012) (the website is closed, but the same information is available at: www.comunidadecuatoriana.com).

and reinstatement of the hearing in a cassation appeal, the process is given to this sort of undue delay that clearly violates various human rights enshrined both in the Constitution of the Republic and in several international conventions to which Ecuador subscribes.

With respect to the criminal doctrine used, this case is a clear example of the application of the theory of the Criminal Law of the Enemy, according to which criminal law is used as a system to discipline or domesticate society, and especially those who do not think a particular way.

It was said that the so-called "pamphlet bombs" that the accused allegedly planned to build and install would have caused an escalation of violence that generated alarm among the populace. From this perspective, the manner in which the authorities organized various press conferences to inform about the raids and detentions had the objective of creating a sense of insecurity among the population in the shape of fear of the harm befalling to others — here, the 10 accused. Thus, though various official news channels, the authorities indirectly placed pressure on the judges and also played with the concept of generating a sense of fear, by presenting the accused as public enemies.

The legal and media handling of this case calls for a deep reflection on the danger that an imbalance of state functions can pose to a democratic society — and in particular, the risks generated by the by the systematic lack of human rights protections when there is no judicial independence in the country.

d. Which Human Rights Were Violated in these

Arbitrary Proceedings, and Why?

The human rights enshrined in the Constitution of the Republic, the Universal Declaration of Human Rights and the American Declaration of Human Rights were violated over the course of more than four years of trial.

In addition, doctrinal principles such as the principle of consistency have been violated[56] because the Criminal Court unexpectedly convicted the accused of an altogether different crime from that for which they had been accused, investigated, charged, and tried.[57]

The lack of judicial independence evidenced by the constant political pressure exerted by public servants on the judges, in this case, makes visible an egregious violation of Article 168.1 of the Ecuadorean Constitution, which provides that "the organs of the Judicial Function shall enjoy internal and external independence."

---

56. "This power, attendant to the principle *iura novit curia*, must be understood and interpreted in harmony with the principle of consistency and the right to a defense. The necessary consistency between the indictment and the possible conviction justifies the suspension of the debate and the new questioning of the defendant, when the factual basis of the indictment wants to be changed. If this occurs irregularly, the right to a defense is damaged, in the measure that the defendant is not able to exercise it with regard to all the facts that will be considered in the judgment." Fermin Ramirez v. Guatemala, Merits, Reparations, and Costs, Inter-Am. Ct. H.R. (Ser. C) No. 126, ¶ 74 (June 20, 2005).

57. "The rigorous regulation of the right to be heard, which we have studied, would make no sense if it did not also provide that the verdict should *only* be issued on the facts and circumstances contained in the charging document, which have been leveled against the accused, and accordingly, on those charging elements on which he has had an opportunity to be heard. This implies forbidding that the verdict extend to facts or circumstances not included in the proceedings afforded by the right to a hearing (*ne eat iudex ultra petita*). This rule is expressed as the *principle of correlation between the charge and the verdict.*" JULIO MAIER, 1 DERECHO PROCESAL PENAL 568 (Editores del Puerto) (2004).

The right to due process enshrined in Article 76 of the Constitution has also been violated, and the following guarantees in particular:

a) The presumption of innocence[58]
b) Evidence duly and lawfully admitted[59]
c) The right to a defense, and specifically: the prohibition of the deprivation of the right to a defense,[60] the right to sufficient time and means to prepare an adequate defense,[61] the right to be timely heard and under conditions of fairness,[62] the right to present evidence and dispute any verbal or written evidence presented against the accused,[63] the right to be tried before an independent, impartial, and competent judge,[64] and the guarantee that state action must be reasoned.[65]

Likewise, minimum guarantees provided under Article 77 of the Constitution, which protects persons deprived of liberty, were also violated as follows:

• Article 77.1 provides that deprivation of liberty will not be the general rule, except in cases of apprehension *in flagrante delicto*; here, however, the accused were not committing any crime when they were detained, but merely participating in a youth meeting.

58. Constitucion de la Republica del Ecuador art. 76.2 (2008).
59. *Id.* at art. 76.4.
60. *Id.* at art. 7.a.
61. *Id.* at art. 7.b.
62. *Id.* at art. 7.c.
63. *Id.* at art. 7.h.
64. *Id.* at art. 7.k.
65. *Id.* at art. 7.1.

- Article 77.3 was violated because the reason for the arrest was not disclosed.
- Article 77.11 was also violated because no alternative interim measures were considered before resorting to pretrial custody.
- Finally, Article 82 of the Constitution, regarding legal certainty, was disregarded.

Likewise, the following principles of the Universal Declaration of Human Rights were violated:

Article 3. The right to liberty.

Article 8. The right to an effective remedy by competent national tribunals

Article 9. The right against arbitrary detention

Article 11. The right to the presumption of innocence

Article 12. The right against arbitrary interference with privacy, family, and home

Article 18. Freedom of thought

Article 20. Freedom of peaceful assembly and association

The following rights under the American Convention on Human Rights[66] were also compromised:

Article 8. Fair trial guarantees

Article 9. Freedom of ex-post facto laws

Article 12. Freedom of conscience

Article.13. Freedom of thought

Article 15. The right of assembly

Article 25. The right to judicial protection

---

66. Organization of American States, American Convention on Human Rights, Nov. 22, 1969, O.A.S.T.S. No. 36, 1133 U.N.T.S.

Other principles were violated that are enshrined in Ecuador's Organic Judicial Code, namely:

The principle of constitutional supremacy, principle of immediate application of constitutional norms, integral principle of the constitutional norm, principle of freedom from ex post facto laws, principles of jurisdiction and competence, principle of independence, principle of impartiality, principle of responsibility, principle of celerity, principle of effective judicial protection, principle of rule of law, principle of procedural truth, principle of compulsory administration of justice, and principle of interpretation of procedural rules.

e. What is the Nature of the Rule of Law in Ecuador Under the Current Constitution?

Since the Constitution of the Republic—drafted by the Constituent Assembly of Montecristi, approved by referendum on September 28, 2008, and published in Official Register Number 449 dated October 20 of that year—took effect; Ecuador went from being a state grounded in the rule of law ("*Estado de Derecho*") to a constitutional state governed by rights and justice ("*Estado Constitucional de Derechos y Justicia*").

To that end, Article 1 of the current Constitution establishes that Ecuador is a constitutional state governed by rights and justice that is social, democratic, sovereign, independent, unitary, intercultural, plurinational and secular. This new governance model focuses on protecting the rights of individuals and groups, recognizing within a pluralist legal framework individuals, communities, peoples, nationalities, and social groups as holders of the rights guaranteed in the Constitution and international agreements.

Rooted in the normative and institutional changes that Ecuador has suffered relentlessly in recent years, any socio-legal analysis of the country's state of affairs must necessarily originate from what the current Constitution provides, particularly with regard to the constitutional rights currently in place.

In that sense, the Constitution establishes, for organizational and logical purposes, a new catalog of rights.[67] This classification provides seven categories of rights, and among those, we concern ourselves here with the rights of freedom and protection.

Rights of freedom — also known as civil rights — include, among others, formal equality, real or material equality, non-discrimination, and the right petition the government for redress of individual and collective grievances and receive a reasoned response. To that end, Article 11.2 of the Constitution provides that all persons are equal; enjoy the same rights, duties, and opportunities; and may not be discriminated against for any reason.

Rights of protection — also known as civil liberties — are those protections that allow all other rights to be exercised free of hindrances or undue obstacles. These include the right to free access to justice; the right to effective legal protection; the right to due process; the right to special protection of victims of violations of rights; the non-applicability of statutes of limitations for crimes internationally considered to be serious or unpardonable; the right to legal certainty, and special protection for do-

---

67. Avila Santamaria, Ramiro, Los derechos y sus garantias. Ensayos criticos 99 (2012)

mestic violence and hate-crime victims and child, teen, elderly, and disabled crime victims.[68]

Finally, Article 70 of the Constitution obligates the State to incorporate mandatory gender-equality policies within the public sector and government plans and programs, as well as generally promoting gender equality.

This backdrop is crucial to understanding the national state of affairs in terms of judicial independence and access to justice — particularly with respect to citizens deprived of their liberty for participating in political dissent and social protest. In those cases, the constitutional achievements of limitations on state power, human rights, constitutional supremacy, and the recognition of various social or identity groups as rights-bearers, all hold little sway.

f. What Role Has the "Constitutional Guaranteeism" Played in the Montecristi Constitution to Protect Human Rights Ratified by Ecuador?

Unfortunately, and to the detriment of the current Constitution, Ecuador's constitutional "guaranteeism" is more often nominal or theoretical, and in practice does not comport with its provisions that aim to place limits on power and defend the rights of citizens against state arbitrariness.

Under those circumstances, judges have a tendency to rule by rote formalistic application of rules based on a classical subsumption method (*"metodo subsuntivo"*).[69]

---

68. *Id.* at 108.

69. Subsumption is the logical operation that unites the hypothetical and abstract judgment, at the normative level, with the decision of the real and concrete case, at the practical level. It differs from the method applied for normative construction, *i.e.*, to subsumptively arrive at the validity of the norm to be applied. *See* Dworkin, Ronald, *Los*

Because they do not have much time for study, and because they are not law professors, their decision-making mechanics remains stuck within a legalistic mold. This is even more so when a key factor in them receiving a positive evaluation is maintaining a high percentage of cases solved or the large volume of case turnover[70] – no matter that, as in the case at hand, this often produces arbitrary results.

No doubt often – and this case is no exception – judges rule without applying all available sources of jurisprudence, and other times follow instructions or directives handed down through administrative channels and even hidden guidelines coming from the judiciary or executive authorities.

g. What are the Consequences of Violating the Separation of Powers in a Nation that Identifies as Democratic?

There is a perception that, in cases where the government interests are at stake, there is certain pressure exerted by other branches of government – especially the Executive – on officers of the court and their careers within the judicial system.

---

derechos en serio 79 (Ariel trans., 7th ed. 2009) [*Taking Rights Seriously.* Cambridge, MA: Harvard University Press, 1977.]; Aldunate Lizana Eduardo, *Aproximacion conceptual y critica al neoconstitucionalismo* [*A conceptual and critical approach towards neo – constitutionalism*] 79 – 102, Revista de derecho Valdivia (Vol. XXIII, no. 1 July 2010), *available at* http://dx.doi.org/10.4067/S0718-09502010000100004.

70. Jalkh, Gustavo, Address on Accountability With Respect to the National Assembly (January 2015) *available at* http://www.funcionjudicial.gob.ec/index.php/es/ saladeprensa/noticias/item/2126-discurso-del-dr-gustavo-jalkh-en-la-rendicion-de-cuentas-frente-a-la-asamblea-nacional.html.

On that front, Ecuador faces grave consequences for disturbing the distribution of powers, because the concentration of power has grown worse, there has been a weakening of democracy, and justice has been politicized, with the consequence of diminishing the principles of independence and impartiality, and which, in turn, has rendered the citizenry defenseless.

In the case at hand, pressure on judicial officers by public servants and the president himself is visible, along with the non-application of the legal rules that allow for a defense of the accused under conditions of fairness and in light of the Constitution.

h. But How Are Human Rights Violated by Using the Judiciary to Silence, Intimidate, and Persecute Citizens?

The most frequent human rights violations perpetrated through the courts are carried out by judges who lack independence or impartiality, because they violate the principles of the administration of justice, fail to respect due process and manipulate procedural mechanisms to generate disproportionate penalties.

It could well be said that we are in the era of the criminal law of the enemy. The case at hand certainly suggests this. Arrest and pretrial detention were ordered to prevent a potential terrorist act that could hypothetically occur in a protest match in the future. The due process rights of the accused were repeatedly violated—especially the right to a proper defense—ultimately resulting in disproportionate penalties.[71]

---

71. In Manuel Cancio Melia's view, "according to Jakobs, the Criminal Law of the Enemy is characterized by three elements: [F]irst, there is a

The criminal law of the enemy is properly applied mainly in the context of terrorism cases. A fundamental problem arises, however, when this theory is applied to the planning of any crime — or worse, as in the case at hand, where although the planning stage was never even reached, a conviction for the attempt is issued nonetheless.

i. What Resources and Options do Victims Have Against This Misuse of Law?

When human rights violations are accompanied by torture and illegal arrest, it is appropriate to refer to international human rights protection systems, such as the inter-American or universal systems.

Moreover, denial of a hearing before an independent or impartial tribunal results may allow the persons affected to bring their case to the Inter-American Human Rights System, to the extent that the violation results in a sham or fraudulent conviction.[72]

5. Conclusions

---

broad advancement of punishability; thus the perspective of the criminal legal system is prospective (reference point: future actions)[.] [As opposed to] — as is more common — retrospective (reference point: the act performed). Secondly, the penalties provided are disproportionately high: in particular, attempt, before reaching the punishability barrier, is not recognized for purposes of reducing penalties. Thirdly, certain procedural guarantees are relativized or even suppressed." JAKOBS, GÜNTHER AND CANCIO MELIA, MANUEL, DERECHO PENAL DEL ENEMIGO 79-81 (2003).

72. "The development of international legislation and case law has led to the examination of the so-called "fraudulent res judicata" resulting from a trial in which the rules of due process have not been respected, or when judges have not acted with independence and impartiality." Carpio-Nicolle v. Guatemala, Merits, Reparations, and Costs, Inter-Am. Ct. H.R. (Ser. C) No. 117, ¶ 131 (Nov. 22, 2004).

The case studied reveals a clear imbalance between the different state powers, as well as an absence of judicial independence, both internal and external. With regard to the lack of external independence, a strong influence and meddling from the Executive into the various institutions involved in the administration of justice is perceptible. That pressure would appear to be exerted by a "super-hero" figure of sorts, pitted against a fictitious enemy — made concrete by media manipulation—that must be fought off by any means necessary to safeguard national security.

Reliant on distorted and capricious interpretations and on grounded on the premises above, the violation of various human rights begins to take shape, where the due process becomes imperceptible, signaling the return of the maxim of authoritarianism, "the State am I."

3
AN UNJUST JUDGMENT AND INFAMOUS CONVICTION
AS POLITICAL INSTRUMENTS TO SEIZE PRIVATE TELEVISION CHANNELS

Jorge Zavala Egas[73]

1. Executive Summary

This article denounces the lack of judicial independence in Ecuador. To establish this, we take the example of the criminal prosecution against the Isaias brothers and others, which also served to justify the subsequent seizure of the media channels TC and GAMAVISION. In those proceedings, the State infringed—in a sloppy and cavalier fashion—the defendants' rights to effective legal protection and a proper defense and failed to respect the due process rights guaranteed under international human rights conventions,[74] as well as the protective norm of the

---

73. Postgraduate professor at Universidades Catolica de Guayaquil y de Cuenca, as well as Universidad de Especialidades Espiritu Santo de Guayaquil y San Gregorio de Portoviejo.

74. "All persons shall be equal before the courts and tribunals. In the determination of any criminal charge against him, or of his rights and obligations in a suit at law, everyone shall be entitled to a fair and public hearing by a competent, independent and impartial tribunal established by law. The press and the public may be excluded from all or part of a trial for reasons of morals, public order (*ordre public*) or national security in a democratic society, or when the interest of the private lives of the parties so requires, or to the extent strictly necessary in the opinion of the court in special circumstances where publicity would prejudice the interests of justice; but any judgment rendered in a criminal case or in a suit at law shall be made public except where the interest of juvenile persons otherwise requires or the proceedings concern matrimonial disputes or the guardianship of children." In-

constitutional right[75] to due process for the determination of the criminal culpability attributed to the accused. That is, the study focuses on the violation of human rights through the State's act of political corruption, carried out with the perverse objective of taking private media channels and in concert with the courts, notwithstanding their subject-matter jurisdiction to prevent the violation of the constitutional and conventional right to due process in the criminal proceedings against the accused.

2. The Facts: On the Hunt for Two Television Channels With National Coverage

The taking of the media channels TC and GAMAVISION from the Isaias family's ownership was a political mission whose goal was their appropriation by the National Government of Ecuador, to thereby increase its control over private media outlets—which was and is a substantial part of the strategy by the adherents of the 21st Century Socialism to exercise power.

President Correa's government decided the convictions of the former administrators of Filanbanco S.A. (among them, the accused) for the crime of peculation, ordering the presiding justices to draw up the necessary rulings to that effect. Peculation was the selected offense

---

ternational Covenant on Civil and Political Rights [ICCRR] art. 14.1, *adopted and opened for signature by* G.A. Res 2200A(XXI) (Dec. 16, 1966). 75. "Every person has the right to free access to justice and the effective, impartial and expeditious protection of their rights and interests, subject to the principles of immediate and swift enforcement; in no case shall there be lack of proper defense. Failure to abide by legal rulings shall be punishable by law." CONSTITUCION DE LA REPUBLICA DE ECUADOR art. 75 (2008). "In all processes where rights and obligations of any kind are set forth, the right to due process of law shall be ensured, including the following basic guarantees ..." *Id.* at art. 76.

for three interrelated reasons: a) it is not time-barred from prosecution; b) it may be judged and sentenced in the absence of the accused; and, last, because c) it provided the legal grounds to extradite the Isaias brothers to the U.S. government—it being one of the crimes provided in the treaty in effect between Ecuador and that country—thereby backing up with concrete action the Ecuadorean government's political discourse against the entrepreneurial class—that is, the "rich."

3. The Political Perversion of the Law

The Government had given its order and it had to be carried out, leaving the judges to reach the desired result in their rulings by —in the absence of any conduct whatsoever consisting of abuse, diversion, or misappropriation of public or private funds—feigning legal reasoning about the existence of those punishable offenses, and further justifying with certain sophistry that private persons could be active subjects of a type of offense that, in 1998, applied only to individuals who held some capacity as public servants or functionaries. That is, the justices had to rule that the interpretation of the wording of the penal code, in reference to peculation, encompassed individuals whose activities were regulated by private law—the only way to convict the Isaias brothers and others as perpetrators of the offense of peculation, because they were not public servants between September and December of 1998.

To that end, the ruling justices proceeded to violate the principles of legality and prior definition of criminal offenses as follows:

a) Distorting the capacity required under the criminal laws to be deemed an active subject of the offense of peculation

To liken the Isaias brothers' conduct to the criminal definition of peculation,[76] the logical-deductive reasoning used in the cassation ruling built as a premise the following statement on page 15:

> "[I]t is true that, in principle, only public functionaries may participate in the crime of peculation; yet nevertheless ... by constitutional mandate and according to article 257, as amended, persons who participated in its perpetration are also responsible for this crime, *even when they lack the aforementioned qualities, and precisely among them are those provided under paragraph three where it refers to the servants of state and private banks ...*"[77]

The premise is false, and is belied by establishing the falsity of the two arguments that underpin it.

a.1) First False Argument

Indeed, no law in effect under the 1998 Constitution or that of 2008 defined among the elements of the offense of pecu-

---

76. The criminal statute in effect in 1998, when the acts imputed to the Isaias brothers occured, which the Judgment also cites, states: "Any servant of public organizations and entities and any individual in charge of a public service who should have abused public or private monies, paper representing them, instruments, securities, documents, personal or real property that are in his possession by virtue of or due to his position, whether the abuse consists of embezzlement, arbitrary disposal or any other similar form, shall be punished with imprisonment." CODIGO PENAL art. 257 (first paragraph). "This provision includes servants handling funds of the Ecuadorian Social Security Institute or of state and private banks" *Id.* at art. 257 (second paragraph). The second paragraph was added by *Decreto Supremo* [D.S.] 1429, *Registro Oficial* [R.O.] 337 (May 6, 1977).
77. Underlining added.

lation, as active subjects, persons who lacked any capacity as public functionaries. Nor are such persons included in the second paragraph (not the third, as the ruling cited in a typographical error) of Criminal Code article 257, in effect during the time when the alleged facts occurred.

Both constitutional laws — that of 1998 and of 2008 — refer to the liability of members of the public sector, and both of them subject public servants to "the penalties provided for the offenses of peculation, bribery, extortion, and illicit enrichment," because public servants are the only individuals defined as active subjects, in a perpetrator capacity, of the types of offenses described in the Criminal Code. Both constitutional texts go on to describe "the prosecutions to pursue [those offenses] and their corresponding penalties" as "not time-barred" and, finally, provide for adjudication "even in the absence of the persons accused." That is, three regulating norms are established, of "penalties," "lack of statute of limitations," and "judgment *in absentia*," whose subjects are persons who, being public servants, may commit those offenses as active subjects — but that "will also apply to those who participate in those offenses, even if they lack the aforementioned qualities." Accordingly, persons who are not public servants and therefore cannot be "perpetrators" of those crimes, but who may "participate in those crimes" — which they could only do as accomplices — can be subject to the "penalties" provided for the offense, along with the "lack of statute of limitations" for its prosecution and sentencing, and can likewise can be "tried *in absentia*." Nevertheless, the constitutional laws do not, under any interpretation, provide that persons who lack any capacity as public servants can be accused as perpetrators of the aforementioned offenses, peculation included.

This shows the falsity of the first argument supporting the premise from which the executive, filtered through the justices, proceeds in the ruling

a.2) Second False Argument

The second argument supporting the ruling's premise is that the second paragraph of Criminal Code article 257 defines among the active subjects of the crime of peculation *"servants who handle funds*[78] of the Ecuadorian Social Security Institute [IESS]or of state and private banks." Clearly, this again refers to the same *public servants*, except who, for some reason, deal with funds of the IESS or the country's private or public financial institutions. The statute expressly refers to those self-same public-sector "servants," who in this case manage social-security and banking funds pursuant to some charge, delegation, or mandate, without doing so "in function or by reason of their charge." Public servants who manage the same funds, but not "in function or by reason of their charge," had to be particularly named within a derived subcategory because they were not embraced within the first paragraph, given that—again—they engage in the defined conduct, "not in function of or by reason of their charge," but rather by performing functions distinct from those inherent to their function or charge. For instance, an attorney employed with the Superintendence of Banks who is provisionally assigned as intervenor or liquidator with a private bank does not act "in function or by reason of his charge" — that is, his

---

78. Underlining added.

function or charge as attorney—when engaging in conduct that falls within the criminal definition of peculation. Accordingly, that behavior does not fall within the scope of the first paragraph, but rather the second, which was created precisely to encompass such cases that, otherwise, would remain unpunished as peculation.

What becomes apparent is that there is no appropriate way to justify a decision to interpret the text of the criminal definition of the offense in effect in 1998, as including as perpetrators of peculation those persons who did not, at the time they engaged in the alleged conduct, hold some capacity as public servants. There is none, because this relates to a special crime that protects as a legal good the efficient activity of public administration in providing public services to the citizens, which is hindered or obstructed by such abusive conduct by the persons involved in managing those funds—and private individuals are generally removed from such administrative activity. If private individuals were to participate in those criminal activities in conjunction with public functionaries, it would be as active subjects of offenses involving conduct consistent with peculation, such as theft; or else as accomplices to, but never principal perpetrators of, peculation.

This shows the falsity of the second argument supporting the premise from which the executive, filtered through the justices, proceeds in the ruling.

It is irrefutable that the justices violated the due process rights enshrined in the principles of legality and prior definition of criminal offenses recognized by our Constitution,[79] given that the justices held as perpetrators of the offense of peculation individuals who did not meet the elements of the definition in effect under Criminal Code article 257 when the accused conduct took place.

b) Irrationally subsuming "misuse," a form of conduct removed from the criminal definition of the offense by the legislature in 1978, under the crime of "peculation"
Because there was no proof whatsoever of abuse, diversion, or misappropriation of the private or public funds managed by the Filanbanco administrators, nor by the Isaias brothers or any other employee or functionary, the judicial maneuvering required of the justices to establish the crime of peculation called for vivid imagination. It was thus that the obedient justices came to absurdly and grotesquely find that the conduct attributed to the Isaias brothers was subsumed under the "abuse" that, according to both the trial and cassation judges, the legislature describes as a type of peculation, in the form of "misuse." At the lower court, the judges, knowing that they had to comply with the executive to save their judicial seats, decided to conceal and disavow that the conduct of "misuse" had been decriminalized by the legislature in 1978[80]; however, because that resulted in clear error, the cassa-

---

79. "In all processes where rights and obligations of any kind are set forth, the right to due process of law shall be ensured, including the following basic guarantees: ..." CONSTITUCIÓN, *supra* note 3, at art. 76. "No one shall be judged or punished for a deed or omission which, at the time of its perpetration, is not legally classified by law as a criminal, administrative or other offense; nor shall a punishment not provided for by the Constitution or law be applied. A person can only be judged by a competent judge or authority and in keeping with the procedures corresponding to each proceeding." *Id.* at art. 76(3).
80 R.O. No. 621 (July 4, 1978).

tion justices had to include it in some shape or form, and to that effect, undertook an interpretive process that will live on in the annals of irrationality and judicial absurdity. Indeed, the trial judgment, as its premise, asserts that the accused:

> "thus breached the provisions under numerals 2, 6, and 7 of the "Stabilization Program"; and in that manner *abused* public funds, that is, the liquidity loans granted by the Central Bank of Ecuador, in the *form of misuse,* for their own benefit, *subsuming their conduct under the offense of peculation defined and penalized under the first and second sections of Penal Code article 257 ...."*

The trial judges did not wish to take notice that the legislature had removed misuse from the criminal definition of peculation.

The cassation justices had to correct this grotesque means of convicting the accused, and did so in a manner that was better reasoned, but likewise erroneous. To bring about that falsehood, the justices' first step was asserting that the legislature's express repeal in 1978 of "misuse" as a form of criminal conduct, was not of an element or descriptive expression containing "misuse" as "concept" of the defined conduct, but merely the "word" that expressed that concept, without eliminating the concept of misuse itself, which had remained in effect as proscribed conduct under the "word abuse." What the justices mean to advance is that: a) the conduct of "misuse" of funds was formulated in the definition of the offense under two words — "misuse" and "abuse"; b) the legislature struck out the first "word," but not the second, that

72

embraced concept of "misuse," which always constitutes an "abuse"; and therefore, c) misuse had always been and never ceased to be understood as a type of conduct criminalized as peculation. The cassation ruling, correcting that of the trial court, asserts that between September and December of 1998, the Isaias brothers committed the crime of peculation in the form of "misuse," which had been struck by legislative repeal as a "word," but not as concept of a criminal conduct that had always been encompassed within the verb "to abuse."

With that irrationality-turned-interpretive exercise, the justices held that the Isaias brothers, by breaching the rules of the "Stabilization Program" through use of funds issuing from the credits granted by the Central Bank to Filibanco, without misappropriating them, did "misuse" them. And although, likewise, there was no diminution of assets for the bank's administration or prejudice to the institutional state lender of those funds, there allegedly was, nonetheless, a criminal "abuse" in the "misuse" committed.

As is evident, this interpretive juggling act is inadmissible from any scientific or legal point of view, given that when the legislature removed from the definition of the offense the word "misuse" — which the cassation justices expressly admit — it eliminated the verbal symbol or expression that identified the "concept" of the conduct of "misuse." If the legislature struck the word "misuse," it was to eliminate the concept of "misuse," and with that, to also remove the conduct from the context where it appeared. Accordingly, "misuse" ceased to exist as a form of criminal abuse, that is, as an element of the crime of peculation. Of course, abuse continued to be a criminal conduct, but only in the forms precisely defined by the legislature, among which misuse no longer numbered. No doubt, the conduct of abusing, in the form of misuse — defined as the application of funds toward different ends than those provided in the executive budget — ceased to be a type of action contemplated under the offense of peculation. It therefore strikes as arbitrary, due to its irrationality, to assert that the conceptual entity of "misuse" continued to exist, despite the repeal of the word and its specific concept, because according to the exegetic jugglers, it remained represented by the generic verbal expression of "abuse" that implicitly embraced it. Without more, against the legislature's express will, the justices included misuse by way of an analogical exercise expressly forbidden by the Constitution and the law — that is, because misuse is a form of abuse, and abuse is the nucleus of the offense, every form of abuse, even if not enumerated by the legislature, is embraced within the offense.

What was accomplished is as incoherent as if the legislature struck the word "delivering" from the context of an offense that was described, namely, as "an act that consists of receiving or delivering," and the interpreter maintained that, despite the repeal, the conduct of "delivering" remained effective as implicit in the word "act," and had not been repealed. The irrationality is crystal clear in both cases, given that the legislature's express will is that repealed term not be an element of the offense — in the first case, "abuse" in the mode of conduct constituting "misuse," and in the second case, the "act" performed in the form of "delivering." In other words: "misuse" had ceased to be a codified form of the crime of peculation since the month of July 1978, and yet the justices recognized it as existing in implicit form.

To conclude, the ruling justice violated the guarantees enshrined in the principles of legality and prior definition of criminal offenses, and arbitrarily and irrationally included within the criminal definition of peculation the conduct of misuse—which had been expressly struck out years before—with the sole objective of fitting to the crime the conduct alleged of the Isaias brothers, convicting them, and keeping the seized media outlets in the power and at the service of the Executive.

4. The Impudent Role of the Constitutional Court Subordinated to the Executive

As the Isaias brothers' proceeded to file complaints, through the appropriate extraordinary actions for protection, for the infringement of their constitutional right to due process, the justices of the relevant chamber held at the jurisdictional phase that because, supposedly, the complaint related only to lack of application or erroneous application of the law:

> "HEARING DENIED, of the action for extraordinary protection … and the case is dismissed."[81]

The Court's error, product of its relationship of obedience to the Executive, is made evident simply by noting that the finding of facts and application of the law in an arbitrary manner by the justices in handing down their ruling to convict the accused, with manifest error equiva-

---

81. *Auto* [Writ] of September 17, 2015 (Case No. 0221-15-EP).

lent to a denial of justice, in violation of the right to a fair trial that respects the guarantees of the presumption of innocence, proper defense, and principles of legality and prior definition of criminal offenses, is precisely the subject of an extraordinary action for protection in Ecuador,[82] and the Court is obligated to substantiate and resolve it.

5. The UN Human Rights Committee and the Violation of the Right to Due Process

In its recent opinion on the matter between the Isaias brothers and Ecuador, the United Nations Human Rights Committee held that it lacked competence to reach the merits of the case, but lit the way toward invalidating the unjust conviction. The explanation lies in that, in its Opinion with respect to communication No. 2244/2013[83], the Committee repeatedly found itself lacking competence to disturb the factual and legal findings of the justices that were the object of the executive's prosecution, by means of its judicial power, against the Isaias brothers. The Opinion did expressly find, however, that no such obstacle exists against adjudicating the right to due process recognized in Article 14.1 of the International Covenant on Civil and Political Rights, if it is shown that judicial arbitrariness occurred. The Opinion states that:

> "The Committee recalls its jurisprudence under which it is incumbent upon the courts of State parties to weigh

---

82. CONSTITUCIÓN, *supra* note 3, at arts. 34 and 437.
83. U.N. Human Rights Committee, Opinion adopted by the Committee under Article 5(4) of the Optional Protocol with respect to communication No. 2244/2013, *approved* June 3, 2016, Doc. CCPR/C/116/D/2244/2013.

the facts and the evidence in each particular case, or the application of internal legislation, unless it should be demonstrated that such weighing or application was clearly arbitrary or tantamount to a manifest error or to the denial of justice."[84]

This amounts to international recognition that no judicial action in the finding of facts or application of the law is exempt from consideration as violating the right to due process as enshrined in our Constitution.[85]

6. Conclusions

Lack of judicial independence, product of meddling by the executive branch, determined the criminal conviction of the former administrators of Filibanco S.A., violating their rights to an effective legal remedy before competent national tribunals under fair conditions, to a fair and public hearing before an impartial tribunal, and to the presumption of innocence — fundamental rights that, like due process, are conventionally and constitutionally recognized.

Specifically, there was a violation of the principles of legality and prior definition of criminal offenses guaranteed under international human rights conventions and the Constitution of the Republic of Ecuador, namely:

1. The Constitution of Ecuador[86] and the international human rights conventions[87] provide that judicial pro-

---

84. *Id.* at ¶ 7.14.
85. *See* CONSTITUCION, *supra* note 3, at art. 76(1).
86. *Id.* at arts. 75 and 76.
87. *See* Universal Declaration of Human Rights art. 10, G.A. Res. 217(III) A, U.N. Doc. A/RES/217(III) (Dec. 10, 1948). *See also* Organi-

ceedings must provide the necessary legal guarantees and proceed under fair, independent, and impartial conditions. The studied case has been characterized by intervention from other branches of government and retroactive application of the law. Once the Supreme Court held that the accused could not be prosecuted for peculation and embraced the Final ruling of Attorney General Mariana Yepez, the case was judicially closed. Regardless, the President of the Republic himself, as well as several assemblymen of his party, publicly voiced their disagreement and called to dismiss and sanction the justices — thus seeking a prosecutorial role for the judicial branch, aiming to control and interfere in chambers whose very nature requires absolute independence. This error provides clear evidence before international and impartial tribunals of the lack of complete fairness and arbitrary intrusion of the executive branch.[88] This not only negatively affects the enjoyment of human rights by the individuals subjected to this prosecution, but also affects society as a whole, given the lack of the system of checks and balances inherent in a democracy.

---

zation of American States, American Convention on Human Rights art. 8, Nov. 22, 1969, O.A.S.T.S. No. 36, 1133 U.N.T.S. *and* ICCRR, *supra* note 2, at art. 14.

88. "The judiciary shall decide matters before them impartially, on the basis of facts and in accordance with the law, without any restrictions, improper influences, inducements, pressures, threats or interferences, direct or indirect, from any quarter or for any reason." Basic Principles on the Independence of the Judiciary art. 2, *endorsed by* G.A. Res. 40/32 (Nov. 29, 1985) *and* G.A. Res. 40/146 (Dec. 13, 1985).

2. The right of every person to an effective remedy before competent national tribunals has been violated.[89] The justices who heard the case were favored in obtaining their seats, by up to 10 points.[90] That was the case of Paul Iniguez and Wilson Merino, who awarded $40 million in damages to compensate alleged harm to Rafael Correa's reputation[91] and sentenced the Isaias brothers to eight years in prison. Iniguez Rios has been denounced by his fellow ideologue Marco Tapia of being one of the justices who handles special cases for the party line, and has also been an advisor to the Alianza Pais assemblyman Vethowen Chica and mayoral candidate for Correa's party. This was the same tribunal[92] that rejected and dismissed the Isaias brothers' appeals. It was also the same justices who infamously substituted the finding of peculation for that of misuse of funds. Accordingly, there could be no effective remedy, with proceedings presided over by justices lacking independence and character and fitness for the bench.

---

89. *See* Universal Declaration, *supra* note 15, at art. 8. *See also* American Convention, *supra* note 15, at art. 8(1).
90. Veeduria Internacional Para la Reforma de la Funcion Judicial de Ecuador, *Informe final de la veeduria internacional para la eleccion de la nueva Corte Nacional de Justicia* [*Final Report of the International Observer of the Elections for a New National Court of Justice*] (Dec. 13, 2012).
91. Enforcement of the final judgment against the newspaper *El Universo* was stayed by intervention of the Inter-American Court of Human Rights, for violating the fundamental human rights of the accused.
92. In which Ximena Vintimilla, Johnny Ayluardo, Jorge Maximiliano Blum y Lucy Blancio also participated.

3. The presumption of innocence has been violated.[93] The facts and evidence show the innocence of the Isaias brothers, and the prosecution has not managed to present evidence supporting charges that Roberto or William Isaias abused Filanbanco or Ecuadorean Central Bank funds to benefit themselves or any third parties. The Inter-American Court of Human Rights requires that no person be convicted without proof of criminal culpability.[94] Meanwhile, the prosecution has also systematically prevented the accused from fully presenting proof of innocence, impeding the presentation of determinative exculpatory evidence, arguments, and documents, and meanwhile failing to itself comply with international standards or the prosecution's own obligation to rely on legitimate and material proof to establish the culpability of the accused.

4. The Isaias brothers did not enjoy, during the period of time when they allegedly committed the suppoesed offenses, that capacity as public servants or functionaries that must necessarily be possessed by those accused as active subjects of the offense of peculation — and yet the justices held otherwise, without justification and contrary to the statutory text.

---

93. *See* Universal Declaration, *supra* note 15, at art. 11(1). *See also* American Convention, *supra* note 15, at art. 8.2 *and* ICCRR, *supra* note 2, at art. 14.2.

94. *See* Cantoral-Benavides v. Peru, Merits, Judgment, Inter-Am. Ct. H.R. (Ser. C) No. 69, ¶ 120 (Aug. 18, 2000) ("If the evidence presented is incomplete or insufficient, he must be acquitted, not convicted.") On the subjects of credible proof of guilt as an indispensable requirement for criminal punishment and that the accused is not required to prove innocence because the burden of proof is on the accuser, *see id.* at ¶¶ 118-128 and Lopez Mendoza vs. Venezuela, Merits, Reparations, and Costs, Judgment, Inter. Am-Ct. H.R. (Ser. C) No. 233, ¶ 128 (Sept. 1, 2011).

5. Because no proof existed of the misuse of the public or private funds handled by the Isaias brothers, the theory of misuse as a form of conduct criminalized as peculation was devised, first, by the trial judges who concealed its repeal in 1978, and, second, by the cassation justices who acknowledged the effective decriminalization of misuse as of that date, but held nonetheless that it continued to exist as a crime, because it remained implicitly effective, as contained within the concept of "abuse" that is the nucleus of the offense of peculation.

6. The Constitutional Court of Ecuador, in an act of political submissiveness, found that the complaint of the accused that they were convicted through an improper application of the criminal definition to which the adjudicated conduct was conformed, was a matter of mere legality, and therefore did not violate the guarantees of the principle of prior definition of criminal offenses or the constitutional right to due process.

7. As we have shown, in the criminal proceeding against the Isaias brothers, to accomplish its political goal of appropriating the media channels the accused owned, the national government first ordered their imprisonment to force them to seek protection abroad, meanwhile calling for their trial so that the justices could carry out in their ruling an arbitrary evaluation of the facts and application of the law, amounting to manifest error and denial of justice.

4
FROM "AUTHOR BY OMISSION" TO PRINCIPAL AND ACCOMPLICE TO SABOTAGE AND TERRORISM FOR "CLAPPING": THE CASE OF FRANCISCO DANIEL ENDARA DAZA

Fabricio Rubianes Morales[95]
Carlos Manosalvas Silva[96]

1. Executive Summary

This study aims to establish the grave infringement of fundamental rights committed through the prosecution of Ecuadorean citizens who think differently from their Government. The study focuses particularly on the case of Francisco Daniel Endara Daza, who, for allegedly clapping in the midst of a social protest outside the facilities of the television channel *Ecuador TV* ("ECTV") on September 30, 2010 (hereafter "30S"), was fined and sentenced to four years in prison. Over the course of five years of litigation and appeals, Endara's charges shifted first from "co-perpetrator" to "accomplice by applause" in the crime of "sabotage and terrorism," and ultimately resulted in his sentencing by the National Court of Ecuador to an 18-month prison sentence as co-perpetrator of

95. Doctor of Jurisprudence, International University of Ecuador; Master in University Teaching and Education Administration; Master's Candidate in Criminal Law and Criminal Procedure at the Central University of Ecuador; and Law Professor at the Central University of Ecuador.
96. Attorney, Central University of Ecuador; Master's in International Negotiation and Foreign Trade; and Master's in International Environmental Law.

the offense of "stoppage of public services,"[97] a different offense than that for which he initially stood accused.

2. Introduction

This analysis concerns the judgment against Francisco Daniel Endara Daza,[98] a human rights victim in Ecuador. The judgment at the trial level violates the right to due process, as well as the right to freedom of expression.[99]

The analysis' main objective is to bring to light how an inapplicable sentence came to be pronounced against an Ecuadorean citizen by fitting his conduct within the definition of a criminal offense in order to establish liability. In this case, mere applause cannot establish the offense of sabotage, let alone its co-commission by Francisco Endara Daza.

3. Factual Narrative and Context of the Case.

The Office of the Attorney General initiated the proceedings in light of the events of the 30S, where a large group of people gathered outside the facilities of the Public Television and Radio Company of Ecuador, *RTV Ecuador* ("ECTV").

---

97. The criminal offense defined in article 346 of the *Codigo Organico Integral Penal* [Integral Organic Criminal Code] [COIP] was used. *Registro Oficial* [Official Register] [R.O.] *Suplemento* [Supplement] 180, Feb. 10, 2014 (Ecuador).
98. *Caso* [Case] No. 17721-2014-1123, Judgment issued by the Specialized Chamber for Criminal, Military Criminal, Police Criminal, and Transit Matters of the National Court of Justice of Ecuador, in case, initiated by the Ecuadorean State through the Office of the Attorney General, for the criminal offense of sabotage, against Francisco Endara Daza and others.
99. *Juicio* [Trial] No. 69-2013, sustained at the trial level by the Second Court of Criminal Guarantees.

The crowds called out for the right to freedom of expression, which was violated that day by ECTV's seizure by government order of all television and radio airwaves in order to broadcast propaganda favorable to the Government—placing the citizens of Ecuador in a state of disinformation about the facts unfolding that day.

According to the prosecution,[100] the large group that approached ECTV—numbering about 200 people—violently entered the premises, disrupting the production and transmission of the public channels. Out of the entire group that the District Attorney's Office identified, only those who had somehow participated in criticizing Rafael Correa's government were prosecuted.

From the outset, a clear persecution was evident against Francisco Endara, whom the prosecution accused as "author by omission" with the notorious aim of linking him to the criminal process. Subsequently, without any element of conviction, the Fifth Judge of the Court of Criminal Guarantees of Pichincha, Dr. Raul Martinez Munoz, ordered trial proceedings[101] for the offense of sabotage, defined in article 158 of the Criminal Code,[102] against Francisco Endara and others, as the alleged perpetrators of the crime of sabotage and terrorism at the premises of the state channel ECTV.

The fifth judge of the Court of Criminal Guarantees of Pichincha suspended the start of the trial phase[103] against

---

100. *Juicio* No. 17721-2014-1123.
101. The trial order was entered on August 26, 2011, by the Fifth Judge of the Court of Criminal Guarantees of Pichincha, Raul Martinez Munoz, Quito, Ecuador.
102. CODIGO PENAL DE ECUADOR art. 158, R.O. No. 147 (Jan. 22, 1971).
103. The order cites the provisions of article 233 of the Code of Criminal Procedure, R.O. No. 360 (January 13, 2000): "Suspension and continuation.- If at the time of issuing the writ of appeal to trial, the

the accused, whose whereabouts were unknown until they were detained or voluntarily appeared at trial. He also denied substitution of the protective order issued against four of the accused, for not having justified their ties to the community.

Appeals for annulment of the order to initiate trial proceedings were rejected by the appellate judges—that is, by the Criminal Division of the Provincial Court of Pichincha[104]—who held there existed no grounds for annulment whatsoever and that any arguments should be advanced in the relevant stage of the proceeding, before the appropriate Criminal Court.

On March 8, 2014, at 13:53 hours, the Second Court of Criminal Guarantees of Pichincha[105] issued the criminal verdict against Francisco Daniel Endara Daza and others, finding them guilty of the offense of sabotage[106] and imposing a prison sentence of:

---

defendant is a fugitive, the penal judge of guarantees after dictating an order, will suspend the trial phase until it is terminated or is submitted voluntarily, except in criminal proceedings relating to offences of embezzlement, bribery, illicit enrichment and theft, in which the proceedings will continue in the absence of the defendant. If there are several defendants, and some are fugitives and other present, the start of the trial will be suspended for the former and will continue with respect to the second."

104. The Criminal Chamber of the Provincial Court, composed of judges Dr. Anacelida Burbano Jativa, President Judge; Dr. Patricio Sanchez Viteri, Commissioned Provincial Judge; and Dr. Jorge Andrade Lara, Commissioned Provincial Judge, by judgment of May 15, 2013, at 11:01 hours, ruled to reject the plea for annulment raised by the accused "because in the trial stage, the materiality of the infringement as well the culpability of the accused must both be shown."

105. The Second Court of Criminal Guarantees Court of Pichincha was composed of judges Dr. Miriam Escobar Perez, President; Attorney Fernando Burbano Davalos, Commissioned Judge; and Dr. Hugo Horacio Aulestia, Commissioned Judge.

106. Codigo Penal, *supra* note 8, at arts. 42 and 158.

"EIGHT YEARS OF MAJOR ORDINARY INCARCER-
ATION each; which sentence, in accordance with article
29, numerals 6 and 7, and in accordance with article 72 of
the Criminal Code, is modified by the sentence of FOUR
YEARS OF MAJOR ORDINARY INCARCERATION."

The defendants were further ordered to pay an $87
fine and $5,000 in reparations for the damage caused.[107]

That judgment was appealed by each of the defendants, establishing jurisdiction before the Criminal
Chamber of the Provincial Court of Pichincha,[108] which
dismissed the appellant's motions and in main part noted:

"… In regard to the defendant Francisco Endara Raza
[sic], this Appeals Court concludes that the accused
Francisco Endara participated in the crime, in the degree of accomplice, because from the evidence presented at the judgment hearing, it was established beyond all doubt that on the day of the punishable act,
the appellant Fernando Endara entered the building in
which the state television channel ECUADOR TV operates; he was among the people who broke down the
glass door, although at no time was he seen destroying
any property - the latter was even expressly stated by
Dr. Gustavo Benitez, Prosecutor of the charge, at the
time when he used the principle of contradiction in
the hearing of the merits of the appeal; prevented the

---

107. Judgment available at http://consultas.funcionjudicial.gob.ec/
informacionjudicial/ public/informacion.jsf.
108. The Chambers of the Provincial Court of Justice of Pichincha was
composed of judges Dr. Luis Emilio Veintimilla Ortega, Dr. Wilson
Lema, and Dr. Marco Rodriguez Ruiz. . [Judgment] of Quito, Thurs-
day, May 29, 2014, at 09:43 hours.

passage of a television camera, as well as people who were on the outskirts of the station premises ; applauded, as clear signal of approval of the protest; and, in some photography, appears next to the accused Pablo Guerrero, all of these prior and simultaneous acts with which, in indirect and secondary manner, he cooperated in the performance of the punishable act, in the terms of article 43 of the Criminal Code; modifies his degree of participation from author to accomplice, reason by which also modifies the sentence of four years ordinary imprisonment to two years of correctional imprisonment." (error in the accused's last name in the original)[109].

The judgment issued by the Criminal Chamber of the Provincial Court of Pichincha is the subject of a Cassation Appeal by Francisco Daniel Endara Daza and others, with jurisdiction lying before the Specialized Chamber in Criminal, Military Criminal, Police Criminal and Transit Matters of the National Court of Justice of Ecuador,[110]

---

109. The name by which Francisco Endara was referred to changed constantly throughout the proceedings; at different times it was Victor Hugo Endara, Fabricio, and Fernando Endara, among others. This shows sloppiness by the operators of justice in this case, and also proof that they lacked any clear understanding of the accused's identity.
110. The Specialized Chamber for Criminal, Military Criminal, Police Criminal and Transit Matters of the National Court of Justice of Ecuador in case No. 17721-20141-123 was made up of the judges Dr. Miguel Jurado Fabara, National Judge-Rapporteur; Dr. Vicente Robalino Villafuerte, National Judge; and Dr. Edgar Flores Mier, National Co-Judge.

which held inadmissible[111] the appeals brought by the defendants Francisco Daniel Endara Daza and others.[112]

The judges of the National Court, purporting to apply the principle of favorability[113] and arguing that "in accordance with International Human Rights Instruments, this Court of Cassation thereby reforms the judgment as elevated in degree," held Francisco Daniel Endara Daza and others as co-perpetrators of the crime of "stoppage of public services,"[114] imposing on each one a sentence of 18 months imprisonment.

From that sentence issued by the Criminal Chamber of the Provincial Court of Pichincha in August 2016, Francisco Daniel Endara Daza appealed to the Constitutional Court, presenting the appropriate action for extraordinary protection,[115] which was denied.[116]

---

111. The judges of the Specialized Chamber for Criminal, Military Criminal, Police Criminal and Transit of the National Court of Justice ruled on November 23, 2015, at 13:15 hours.

112. In addition to Francisco Endara Daza, the other defendants were: Victor Hugo Erazo Rodriguez, Patricio Tonny Fajardo Larrea, Marcelo Max Marin Guzman, and Galo Efren Monteverde Castro.

113. Principle of favorability is provided in the Constitution of the Republic, specifically in COIP arts. 76.5, 5.2, and 16.2.

114. "Stoppage of a public service.- Any person who prevents, hinders or paralyzes the normal provision of a public service or violently resists the restoration of the same; or takes by force a building or public facility, shall be punished with imprisonment of one to three years." COIP art. 346.

115. "The extraordinary action for protection takes as an object the protection of the constitutional rights and due process in judgments, definitive orders, resolutions with the force of judgment, that have been violated by action or omission rights recognized in the Constitution." *Ley Organica de Garantias Jurisdiccionales y Control Constitucional* [Organic Law of Jurisdictional Guarantees and Constitutional Controls] art. 58, R.O. No. 52 (Oct. 22, 2009).

116. "SERIOUS INFRINGEMENTS.- The servant of the Judicial Function shall be liable by penalty of dismissal, for the following disciplinary infractions: 7. For intervening in the proceedings that he or she must operate, as Judge, district attorney or public defender, with

4. Sentence Issued Against Francisco Endara Daza

In the proceedings prior to the cassation appeal, several of the judges who intervened did so in a capacity as temporary appointees and, seeking some stability in their appointments, did not rule according to law. Similarly, the permanent judges, out of reverential fear of the Government, preferred not to contradict the regime's perverse goals, as that could cost them the elimination of their judicial functions under the guise of discipline by the Judiciary Council, under the infamous doctrine of inexcusable error[117] – more than sufficient grounds to hand down a sentence contrary to law and far removed from the reality of the facts and circumstances.

Flagrant violations of due process occurred. One is that there was never a positive identification of the suspects[118] (now the condemned).[119] There is no record in the case file substantiating that the appropriate due diligence of positively identifying the defendants was performed.

---

fraud, clear negligence or inexcusable error ..." Organic Code of the Judicial Function [Codigo Organico de la Funcion Judicial] art. 109.7.

117. Any judge in Ecuador can be denounced for errors deemed "inexcusable," specifically those that violate constitutional norms and due process in any judicial process. The problem is that "inexcusable error" can be interpreted ambiguously and subjectively.

118. In accordance with *Codigo Procesal Penal* [Code of Criminal Procedure] arts. 80 and 216.7 and Constitucion de la Republica de Ecuador art. 74.6 (2008).

119. The positive identification of suspects subjected to criminal proceedings, according to the criminal laws in effect at the time of the events (Oct. 30, 2010), was to perform that diligence in the presence of defense counsel; before the judge of criminal guarantees, the secretary, and the injured party; and with the use of a Gesell chamber, where the suspect is displayed in the company of ten other similarly dressed people. Once positive identification is complete, it is reported in the record with the signature of the judge, the Secretary, and the person who identified the suspect.

But it was the very witnesses who testified that they had not personally seen Francisco Endara Daza inside the channel ECTV. Likewise, no witness could identify Francisco Endara committing any act of destruction inside ECTV. The witnesses said they had only recognized Francisco Endara in the videos presented, that his demeanor was peaceful, and that his name had been provided to them by the prosecution, in violation of every principle of independence, impartiality, and the presumption of innocence.[120] This was evident at the hearing before the Second Court of Criminal Guarantees, confirmed by the Criminal Chamber of the Provincial Court, where all witnesses (employees and officials of Ecuador TV) said they recognized the accused in videos presented as evidence at the hearing—in violation of the due process provided under the Constitution of the Republic of Ecuador.[121]

None of the witnesses directly saw Francisco Daniel Endara Daza gathered at *Avenida De los Shyris, Aveni-*

---

120. *See* article 14.2 of the International Covenant on Civil and Political Rights ("Every person accused of an offense has the right to be presumed innocent until proved guilty according to law."). *See also* Marti de Mejia v. Peru, Case 10.970, Report No. 5/96, Inter-Am. Comm. H.R. (1996) *and* Loayza-Tamayo vs Peru, Merits, Inter-Am. Ct. H.R. (Ser. C.) No. 33 (Sept. 17, 1997).

121. "In all processes where rights and obligations of any kind are set forth, the right to due process of law shall be ensured, including the following basic guarantees: ... The right of persons to defense shall include the following guarantees: a) No one shall be deprived of the right to defense at any stage or level of the proceedings. b) To have the time and means to prepare for one's defense. c) To be listened to at the right time and with equal conditions. h) To submit verbally or in writing the reasons or arguments of those who are being assisted and to respond to the arguments of the other parties; to submit evidence and challenge the evidence that is submitted against them. CONSTITUCION, *supra* note 24, art. 76.7(a) − (b),(h).

da Eloy Alfaro, or *Avenida Republica*—let alone inside the premises of *Ecuador TV;* accordingly, there is no evidence of the conspiracy to commit any crime.

5. Constitutional Violations Carried in the Judgments Against Francisco Endara Daza

The Specialized Chamber of the Criminal Court of the National Court of Justice, in its judgment,[122] after five years of litigation, violated the constitutional guarantee of due process. Its ruling, in section 7.2.7, pursuant to the principle of favorability[123] and its application in criminal matters, replaces the criminal offense of sabotage[124] for that of obstruction of public service,[125] erratically stating that the conduct is still punishable, notwithstanding that the objective and subjective elements of those criminal offenses are completely different, and their operative verbs are even more so.[126]

The objective elements of the criminal offense established in the obstruction of public service[127] do not include causing social alarm, nor do they have the same operative verbs as sabotage, therefore the norm transgressed in breach of the principle of legality and rule of law that must be protected in all legislation.

---

122. Sentence issued by the Specialized Criminal Court of the National Court of Justice on November 23, 2015, at 13:15 hours.

123. COIP at art. 5(2).

124. *See* CODIGO PENAL, *supra* note 8. It is important to clarifiy that Franciso Endara Daza was punished under the 1971 code and not under the COIP, which was adopted February 10, 2014.

125. COIP art. 346, R.O. Sup. No. 180 (Feb. 10, 2014).

126. The operative verbs of the definition sabotage are: destroy, deteriorate, disable, disrupt, paralyze. *See* CODIGO PENAL, *supra* note 8, at art. 158.

127. COIP art. 346.

It should be noted that judicial authorities are obligated in a criminal proceeding to compare the facts with the specific offense defined by law. In this case, the mere presence of Francisco Endara Daza at ECTV does not even closely fit the crime of which he is accused. With respect to likening a person's conduct to a criminal offense defined by law, the Inter-American Court of Human Rights indicates that "it is incumbent upon the criminal judge, upon applying criminal law, to strictly abide by the provisions thereof and be extremely rigorous when likening the accused person's conduct to the criminal definition, so as not to punish someone for acts that are not punishable under the legal system."[128]

Article 76 of the Constitution clearly speaks of the due process that must have in all proceedings, and particularly those of criminal in nature, by virtue of which is at stake the most precious legal good of the human being: freedom.

That freedom is enshrined not only in the Constitution of the Republic, but also in international treaties and conventions like the International Covenant on Civil and Political Rights,[129] the Universal Declaration of

---

128. Garcia Asto and Benavides Rojas v. Peru, Preliminary Objection, Merits, Reparations, and Costs, Inter-Am. Ct. H.R. (Ser. C.) No. 137 ¶ 190 (Nov. 25, 2005). *See also* Case Fermin Ramirez v. Guatemala, Judgment, Merits, Reparations, and Costs, Inter-Am. Ct. H.R. ¶. 90 (June 20, 2004); and, Case De la Cruz Flores v. Peru, Judgment, Merits, Reparations, and Costs, Inter-Am. Ct. H.R. ¶ 82. (Nov. 18 2004).

129. International Covenant on Civil and Political Rights [ICCRR] art. 19.1 and 19.2, *adopted and opened for signature by* G.A. Res 2200A(XXI) (Dec. 16, 1966) ("1. Everyone shall have the right to hold opinions without interference. 2. Everyone shall have the right to freedom of expression...").

Human Rights,[130] and the American Convention on Human Rights "Covenant of San Jose de Costa Rica."[131] That freedom was infringed by the Judicial Administration of the Ecuadorean State by condemning Francisco Endara Daza to 18 months of imprisonment and payment of an "integral reparation," on account of thinking differently from the incumbent Government, for posing next to an accused of greater political statute and—the most *avant garde* reason in our jurisprudence—for "applauding."

In light of the clear violations of the right to due process established in article 76 of the Ecuadorean Constitution (i.e., first, binding a person to criminal proceedings by stretching the law to charge him of "commission by omission"; second, convicting him without more evidence than merely being present at a particular place and time in a demonstration against the incumbent government to advocate for freedom of expression; third, by altering the judgment to convict him as an accomplice for "applauding"; and finally, by sentencing him as the perpetrator of a crime different from that for he was initially charged and prosecuted) the action for extraordinary protection was brought—the same motion described above, whose filing was rejected. This clear judicial persecution makes evident the incumbent government's political interest in

---

130. *See* Universal Declaration of Human Rights art. 19, G.A. Res. 217(III) A, U.N. Doc. A/RES/217(III) (Dec. 10, 1948) ("Every individual has the right to freedom of opinion and of expression…").

131. *See* Organization of American States, American Convention on Human Rights art. 13.1, Nov. 22, 1969, O.A.S.T.S. No. 36, 1133 U.N.T.S. ("1. Everyone has the right to freedom of thought and expression. This right includes freedom to seek, receive, and impart information and ideas of all kinds, regardless of frontiers, either orally, in writing, in print, in the form of art, or through any other medium of one's choice…").

using the justice system to pursue and to silence critics, in violation of articles 14.1 and 26 of the International Covenant on Civil and Political Rights.[132]

6. Fundamental Aspects of the Alleged Criminal Culpability

The objective elements of the criminal offense charged, defined in Criminal Code article 158, were never met by the accused's conduct, since the operative verbs of destroying, deteriorating, disabling, disrupting, and paralyzing were never carried out or performed by Francisco Daniel Endara Daza, and his conduct never resembled those actions.

Those behaviors have as their object "the facilities of radio, telephone, telegraph, television or any other system of transmission"[133] — and in the words of the manager of ECTV: "Thank God, the signal of ECTV was never interrupted."

---

132. *See* ICCRR art. 14.1 ("All persons are equal before the courts and tribunals. Every person shall have the right to be heard publicly and with the due guarantees by a competent, independent and impartial court established by the law, in the substantiation of any accusation of a criminal nature made against him or for the determination of his rights and obligations of a civil nature.") *and id* at art. 26 ("All persons are equal before the law and are entitled without any discrimination to the equal protection of the law. In this respect, the law shall prohibit any discrimination and will guarantee to all persons equal and effective protection against discrimination on any grounds such as race, color, sex, language, religion, political opinion, or of any nature, national or social origin, economic position, birth or any other social condition").

133. Codigo Penal, *supra* note 8, at art. 158.

The operative verbs and their established object have an intended purpose or result, which is to produce a collective alarm.[134]

What is clear is that it was never shown, at any stage of the proceedings, that Francisco Daniel Endara Daza at any point participated in:

• damaging the external iron door of the ECTV station;
• breaking the screen and glass door;
• breaking windows; or
• damaging or rupturing wires or a fixed screen (whose breakage by the kick of a citizen is clearly visible, but difficult to identify by the prosecution and less so by the Private Accuser, let alone by members of the Judicial Police — clearly showing the existence of political persecution in this case and the subordination of justice to the government in power).

It is also important to emphasize that, as it relates to these proceedings, Francisco Daniel Endara Daza did not assault any person or bystander witness, let alone the accuser. His presence was rather that of a peacemaker, as it was established at the appellate level (second instance).

It was never proved that Francisco Daniel Endara Daza ever shouted neither in favor of the regime, nor against it, and neither against the public company of ECTV.

Francisco Daniel Endara Daza never set foot on the news set nor in the master control room of the TV station.

---

134. The collective alarm on 30S, at issue here, was sparked since 07:30 hours, and not as a result of the turn of events at ECTV premises. *See* Appendix, *infra*.

The only "sin" of Francisco Daniel Endara Daza, according to the District Attorney, the Private Prosecution, and the Judicial Police, is to have clapped (a fact that also was never shown at trial), just as the hundreds of people in the vicinity of the ECTV premises clamoring for freedom of expression also did. It is also worth asking: why were only 13 people charged, when at least two hundred people were present outside the ECTV station? Is clapping a crime?

The record does not remotely establish any causal link that might support the assertion that Francisco Daniel Endara Daza is responsible for the alleged sabotage codified in Criminal Code article 158.

Doctrine and jurisprudence hold that, to establish both the materiality and the responsibility in this type of crime, the defendant must have acted with malice; this was never established by the prosecution, and even less by the accuser.

The judicial protection is an obligation that the judges must have in all their resolutions, but the performance of the judges of the Specialized Chamber of the Criminal Court of the National Court of Justice[135] shows their lack of knowledge, to say the least, of the rule contained in article 25.1 of the American Convention on Human Rights.[136]

---

135. Conformed by: Dr. Miguel Antonio Jurado Fabara; Dr. Vicente Robalino Villafuerten and Dra. Zulema Pachacama Nieto.

136. American Convention, *supra* note 37, at art. 25.1 ("Everyone has the right to simple and prompt recourse, or any other effective recourse, to a competent court or tribunal for protection against acts that violate his fundamental rights recognized by the constitution or laws of the state concerned or by this Convention, even though such violation may have been committed by persons acting in the course of their official duties.").

Likewise, whether without further explanation or merely out of ignorance, they failed to apply the Mandatory Resolution of the Constitutional Court for the transitional period regarding the right to effective judicial protection—*i.e.*, that every judge has the obligation to protect the rights and warranties of every person in a judicial proceeding.[137]

7. Conclusions

The case of Francisco Endara Daza clearly demonstrates the government's abuse of the judicial system to persecute its opponents and critics. Francisco Endara had been active in the spheres of academia and opinion before 30S, voicing critical views regarding the handling of human rights and of economic and political conditions in Ecuador.

30S was simply used as an excuse by the government to persecute its critics, through judicial means. This is evident in the case at hand, as it is clear from the outset of the prosecution how creatively and forcibly legal concepts were manipulated to prosecute Francisco Endara.

That persecution was evident from the start, by the fact that he was initially accused as a "perpetrator by omission."[138] He was then convicted by the trial court as

---

137. *See* R.O. No. 159 (March 26, 2010), publishing the ruling in Case 0041-09-EP.

138. Only a person who has a legal obligation to stop a crime from occurring can accuse as a perpetrator by omission. "In the case of Francisco Daniel Endara—who in the videos offered as evidence by the prosecution appears entering the station peacefully after the door had already been broken down—commission 'by omission,' which article 12 of the Criminal Code provides for that who does not prevent an incident when has the legal obligation to prevent it, the prosecution's charge is incomprehensible." PASARA, LUIS, DUE PROCESS OF LAW FOUNDATION, EXECUTIVE REPORT, *INDEPENDENCIA JUDICIAL EN LA REFORMA DE LA JUS-*

the perpetrator of the crime of sabotage, for which there was not a shred of evidence against him. The persecution continued in the court of appeals (second instance), where the pressure on the judges to condemn Francisco Endara for applauding, despite their recognition that "his role did not correspond to that of either author or agitator," is evident.

It was thus that all national, international, and human rights norms with respect to the right to a fair trial, judicial impartiality, proportionality of punishment, and the presumption of innocence were infringed in this case.

The lack of proportionality with respect to the alleged conduct and the sentence issued is evident in this case (an applause resulting in two years in jail?). Instead, we can see a disregard and disrespect for a person's fundamental rights over the simple fact of having been present in the vicinity of a location where acts of repudiation against the government took place. This indicates that the State played the role of seizing the fundamental rights of a citizen, which is unthinkable in a society that claims to respect the rights of persons.[139]

TICIA ECUATORIANA. [JUDICIAL INDEPENDENCE IN ECUADOR'S JUDICIAL REFORM PROCESS] 10 (2014), *available at* dplf.org/sites/default/files/indjud_ecuador_informe_esp.pdf.
139. FERRAJOLI, LUIGI. PRINCIPIA IURIS. 1 THEORY OF LAW AND DEMOCRACY 720 (2011).

Appendix: Brief Chronology of the Facts that Occurred in Quito on September 30, 2010[140]

- 07:30 hours: Approximately 500 members of the police force take the Quito 1 Regiment, the main police station in Quito, the capital of Ecuador. The officers said their actions were in protest of the Organic Law of the Public Service, approved the night before by the National Assembly, which reportedly curtailed their economic benefits.
- 09:00 hours: Sectors of the Armed Forces take to the streets of Quito in support of the police.
- 09:40 hours: President Rafael Correa visits the Quito 1 Regiment to meet with the insubordinate police officers, but fails to establish a dialogue and is attacked. He is carried to the Police Hospital, next door to the Regiment, due to a recent operation to his right knee in which he received an implant. He receives medical treatment but, once recovered, he is informed that he will not be allowed to leave the hospital until the Law of Public Service is repealed.
- 10:05 hours: Police and military occupy the runway of Quito's Mariscal Sucre Airport, preventing the departure and arrival of national and international flights.
- 10:24 hours: There is talk that the President of Ecuador has been kidnapped by members of the National Police.

140. Press Release, Permanent Assembly for Human Rights of Ecuador, *Permanent Assembly for Human Rights of Ecuador Denounces and Demands Penalties of Human Rights Violations by Members of the National Police During the Events of September 30* (Oct. 1, 2010), *available at* http://frentepopularsds.blogspot.ca/2010/10/apdh-del-ecuador-re-procha-y-pide.html.

- 11:00 hours: Ecuador is left unprotected; banks, stores, shopping centers, and other businesses close; and classes are declared suspended until further notice. Chaos begins to erupt in the city.
- 11:30 hours: Demonstrations in support of President Correa erupt throughout the nation's capital.
- 12:30 hours: In a telephone declaration, President Rafael Correa speaks of an attempted coup, accusing Ecuador's former president and ex-Army Gen. Lucio Gutierrez of backing the police insubordination and complaining that violent police officers are trying to enter the hospital room where he is being held.
- 13:00 hours: Citizens begin to mobilize outside the National Police Hospital where the president is being held, hoping to rescue him. Unarmed citizens, members of the presidential cabinet, state authorities, public servants, and other arrive. Brutal police repression begins, with tear gas canisters thrown at the civilian population trying for hours to reach the hospital door.
- 13:30 hours: The Legal Secretary of the Presidency of the Republic calls in a press conference for the Armed Forces to take control of the situation and of the Commander in Chief's safety.
- 13:50 hours: A state of emergency is declared throughout the Ecuadorean territory for five-day period.
- 14:30 hours: The Joint Command of the Armed Forces in a press conference urges the National Police to depose certain elements of the Police and the Armed Forces, calling for sanity and resolution of the conflicts through dialogue.
- 17:30 hours: Military leadership and the Minister of Defense arrive at the Quito airport to dialogue with the

military troops. Airport activities resume definitively at 19:40 hours.

- 21:00: An operation begins with 700 members of the armed forces who enter the Police Hospital to evacuate the President of the Republic amid crossfire that kills a member of the police special group guarding the vehicle that carried the President.
- Others: In the absence of public safety forces in the country's streets, dozens of cases of theft, looting, and other criminal activity are registered, leaving behind thousands of dollars in losses.

It was not the events that unfolded at the ECTV premises that caused widespread alarm. By that time, 18:30 hours, the nation was already convulsing.

V
THE RELATIONSHIP BETWEEN GOVERNMENT AND CIVIL SOCIETY, AND THE (AB)USE OF CRIMINAL LAW IN ECUADOR

AN ILLUSTRATIVE CASE: THE 29 OF SARAGURO

by Rafael Paredes Corral

1. Executive Summary

This analysis examines irregularities in the legal proceedings in the case of "the 29 of Saraguro." In that case, in response to protests on various issues against the National Government, members of the indigenous community of Saraguro were severely repressed and 31 of them arrested. Those citizens were prosecuted and received a disproportionate sentence of four years in prison for the offense of stoppage of public services. This case illustrates the persecution faced by social and indigenous leaders who have been denied their rights of assembly, protest, resistance, and due process. Such use of malicious criminal proceedings for political purposes has become a common practice in Ecuador, where the government habitually resorts to criminalizing social protest and disproportionately exercising state power to punish and silence its critics.

2. Introduction

The Ecuadorian central government's relationship with civil society has been highly confrontational. The government has used various tactics to purportedly resolve that conflict—on occasion making certain conciliatory efforts, [141] but ultimately by means of excessive use of police powers and by asserting control over the country's judicial apparatus and all related entities and agencies, which it sought to accomplish on June 4, 2013, with Executive Decree 16. [142]

In this context, the central government's relationship with the indigenous movement has been particularly controversial. Various indigenous communities have often engaged in public protest, as in the case analyzed here. This confrontation has materialized—among other venues—within the criminal justice system, where charges have been filed against those who speak out against the Government on the streets

The criminal prosecution of demonstrators and social leaders has been used as a means of intimidation, to discourage future protests. In this context, criminal proceedings are a mechanism to punish those who publicly speak out against the Government—that is, prosecution itself becomes a punishment imposed even before any sentence is issued. Through that mechanism, defendants are deemed and treated as dangerous criminals, as suggested by the Attorney General Office's use of motions to impose interim measures such as pretrial detention.

---

141. In the national dialogues resulting from protests over proposed estate and capital gains legislation, the central government sought a reconciliation with civil society by amending those laws through Decreto Ejecutivo [Executive Order] No. 739 (Aug. 3, 2015), *published* Registro Oficial [R.O.] [Official Register] No. 570 (Aug. 21, 2015).
142. Decreto Ejecutivo No. 16, *published* R.O. Suplemento No. 19 (June 20, 2013).

That same mechanism operated in the case at hand. A group of members of the Saraguro indigenous community participated in an August 2015 demonstration on the Pan-American Highway. According to available accounts, the National Police used excessive force to violently arrest 31 Saraguro community members. The Saraguro District prosecutor (the "local prosecutor") accused them of participating in the stoppage of a public service,[143] an offense defined under the Comprehensive Organic Criminal Code (hereinafter, "COIP") that carries a prison sentence of one to three years.[144]

After an almost a year of pre-trial proceedings, the 29 defendants appeared in two groups before a local judge. The judge of the Multicompetent Judicial Unit based in the Saraguro District, summoned 22 members of the

---

143. Multicompetent Judicial Unit based in the Saraguro District, Province of Loja; Proceeding No. 11313-2015-00435, for the infraction of Stoppage of Public Services. Injured Parties: Torres Saldana Diego Jose, Dr. Miguel Angel Condolo Poma, Prosecutor; Accused: Macas Ambuludi Atahualpa Yupanky Lima Medina Julio Aurelio; Cartuche Quizhpe Jose Manuel Sarango Quizhpe Julio Aurelio; Lozano Gualan Julio Cesar; Tene Gonzalez Manuel Asuncion; Lozano Gualan Jaime Rodrigo; Ortega Cango Angel Benigno; Zhunaula Sarango Asuncion; Angamarca Morocho Kind Service; Suquilanda Guaman Cesar Martin; Macas Minga Nestor Oswaldo; Lozano Gualan Jose Lino; Lozano Quizhpe Fausto Enrique; Medina Puglla Digner Patricio; Sargo Cango Abel; Andrade Zhingre Marco Vinicio; Medina Quizhpe Angel Polivio; Content Contented Sisa Pacari; Lozano Guaman Sisa Carmen; Cango Medina Teresa De Jeses; Lozano Gualan Rosa Mercedes; Medina Lozano Natividad Maria; Monteros Paguay Karina Fernanda; Minga Gueledel Tania Mariana; Minga Minga Carmen Delfina; Lozano Quizhpe Maria Luisa; Medina Cartuche Carmen Rosaura; Lozano Contento Laura Albertina; Tene Guaillas Light Macrina. Judge: Alex Damian Torres Robalino.

144. COIP art. 346, *published* R.O. No. 180 (Feb. 10, 2014) ("Any person who impairs, obstructs, or paralyzes the regular provision of a public service or violently resists the restoration thereof; or who takes a public building or facility by force; shall be punished by imprisonment for one to three years.").

Saraguro community to proceed to trial. One group of defendants has proceeded to the trial phase before the Loja Court of Criminal Guarantees (the "Criminal Court"), while a second group still awaits an Evaluation and Preliminary Hearing before the Saraguro local judge. Of the first group, all but two have since been acquitted. The remaining two defendants were sentenced to four years in prison, and are still entitled to file a cassation appeal before the National Court of Justice. A cassation appeal allows only a review for error in the application of law, but not a *de novo* review of the facts.

In the course of about one year, the have been driven at the government's instigation, which reveals an unhealthy interest in obtaining exemplary penalties.

3. Abuse of Pretrial Detention

The violation of due process can be seen, first, in the local judge's order for pretrial detention of the 29 at the hearing to determine flagrancy[145]. Although the Ecuadorean Constitution reserves pretrial detention as an exceptional measure,[146] there is no indication in the local court's order that it considered alternative measures instead of pretrial

---

145. The judge ordered pretrial detention at the hearing to determine flagrancy on August 17, 2015, where it asserted jurisdiction as the court sitting in the district of Saraguro. *See* Proceeding No. 11313-2015-00435, *supra* note 4.

146. The Constitutcion de la Republica de Ecuador [Constitucion] (2008) provides, at article 77, numeral 1, that "Deprivation of liberty shall be imposed as an exceptional measure when necessary to guarantee the appearance in the proceedings, or to ensure compliance with the sentence; [it shall] issue by written order of a competent judge, in the cases, for the period of time, and with the formalities provided by law. This does not apply to flagrant offenses, in which cases the detained person may not be held without trial for more than 24 hours. The judge may always order interim measures different from pretrial detention."

detention to ensure the defendants' appearance at trial. Moreover, at the time of the hearing to determine flagrancy it was unknown whether, if convicted, the prison sentence would exceed a year, as is required by law in order to apply pretrial detention.

It should also be noted that the order lacked any of the legal reasoning or factual grounds required to justify incarceration as a means to ensure the presence of the defendant at trial. Most of the detainees live with their families in Saraguro and work in the surrounding area, which makes improbable that they would not obey a court summons (that is, due to each defendant's ties to his or her community, employer, and family). The order belies the local judge's specific intent to satisfy the expectations of the prosecution and police.

The pretrial detention order was appealed to the Specialized Criminal Chamber of the Loja Criminal Court of Justice (the "Criminal Court").[147] The Criminal Court determined that the local judge did not properly reason his decision.[148] Nevertheless, the Criminal Court remanded

147. In their pretrial detention appeal, the defendants argued that the order lacked legal reasoning. It was performed at the flagrancy qualification hearing and the local judge granted it on August 20, 2015, and indicating that, by law, the order would not be suspended while the court considered the appeal. Namely, the local judge held that "no pretrial detention order issued will be suspended because Article 520 (6) of the Comprehensive Criminal Code expressly prohibits it." Proceeding No. 11313-2015-00435, *supra* note 4.

148. In Resolution No. 435-2015, dated September 4, 2015, the Criminal Court held: "In the present case, there is no reasoning whatsoever regarding compliance with the requirements for pretrial detention— specifically, those provided under paragraphs 1, 2 and 3 of Article 534 of COIP; C) .- That is, with respect to the first requirement, regarding the elements of proof for a crime of a public nature, the local judge speaks very generally about it, in that he does not even indicate the circumstances of the place, mode, and time they would have occurred.

the order for further legal analysis, but did not terminate the criminal proceedings because it considered that the errors in the order could be remedied, and cited certain legal precedents to that effect.[149] Thus, the Criminal Court in a sense validated the local judge's error by allowing the criminal proceedings to continue, even though they had not been carried out according to Constitutional requirements.

In this way, the trial court flippantly handled a ruling by the trial court that deprived citizens of their liberty, even if in a preliminary and preventive manner, in order to maintain the integrity of his decision—not only a contradiction in logic, but also an unconstitutional act.[150]

The defendants requested that the local judge replace pretrial detention with alternative measures. He decided to consider the petition only after the Criminal Court had resolved the appeal of pretrial detention order. Then, backpedaling, the local judge summoned a hearing for the petition pursuant to Article 75 of the Constitution.[151]

The same goes for the second requirement, that is, on whether the accused are authors or accomplices of the alleged crime, since the local judge states that there are versions and an informative report on the issue, without indicating who made those declarations or what they declared, nor indicating either what are the acts attributed to each and every one of the appellants, as it should be if it is considered that the Law speaks of clear and precise elements of proof."

149. The Criminal Court's decision remanding the pretrial custody order to the trial court for further legal analysis was issued on September 4, 2015, at which point the defendants had been detained for 19 days. Proceeding No. 11313-2015-00435, *supra* note 4.

150. It should be remembered that an action or omission by government authority that curtails rights is considered contrary to the Constitution. *See* CONSTITUCION, *supra* note 7, at art. 11(8), second paragraph.

151 *Id.* at art. 75 ("Every person has the right to free access to justice and the effective, impartial and expeditious protection of their rights and interests, subject to the principles of immediate and swift enforcement; in no case shall there be lack of proper defense. Failure to

At the hearing held on August 31, 2015, the judge reviewed his decision and replaced pretrial detention with
alternative measures, because the defendants' ties to the
community were verified and the crime for which they
stood accused carries a sentence of less than five years.[152]

4. Local Court ("Primera Instancia")

The proceedings carried on, and the necessary steps in
the main prosecution were taken. Government authorities became involved in the proceedings, however, when
the Ministry of the Interior's Legal Coordinator and the
National Director of the National Police's Legal Counsel
pressed charges as private parties against the defendants.
The Ministry of the Interior official was named common
attorney for the government agencies. As private petitioners, the Ministry of the Interior and the National Police received notifications of case activity. That way, the
Government kept aware of the developments in the case
and could actively participate in the proceedings.

The local judge summoned the defendants to a Preliminary and Preparatory Hearing held November 26,
2015, where, in addition to the private petitioners, the Attorney General's Office also appeared.

At the first hearing, the local prosecutor charged 10
of the defendants with the crime of participating in the
stoppage of a public service. The local judge at that hearing decided to summon those defendants to trial as principals in the first degree. In a sparse written opinion, the

---

abide by legal rulings shall be punishable by law.")
152. The measure of pretrial detention was replaced for all except one,
due to inconsistencies in the documentation justifying their ties to the
community.

local judge limited himself to agreeing with the prosecutor, citing two authors for their doctrine, and concluding that the defendants participated in the degree of co-principals in the crime. The local judge informed the Court of Criminal Guarantees of the trial summons for that cohort of defendants.

At the same hearing, the local prosecutor moved to dismiss charges against 21 defendants. Shortly thereafter, the Loja provincial prosecutor unexpectedly revoked the local prosecutor's dismissal of charges for 19 of those defendants (the provincial prosecutor did ratify dismissal of two defendants' charges).[153]

Upon the revocation of the dismissal by the provincial prosecutor a new preliminary hearing was held from May 20 to May 23, 2016, for those 19 defendants. Accordingly, the charges against those 19 defendants remained in place.

At that second hearing, citing the same laws and doctrines as with the first group of defendants, the local judge summoned to trial 12 of the 19 defendants, and dismissed charges against seven others. Again, the judge notified the Court of Criminal Guarantees of the trial summons for this second group of defendants.

---

153. COIP, *supra* note 5, at art. 600, final paragraph (if "the prosecutor decides to press charges against some but dismiss charges against other defendants, he or she must raise the dismissal for consultation according to the provisions of this article. And with respect to those who are charged, [the prosecutor] shall ask the judge to set the date and time for the pre-trial evaluation and preparatory hearing." In the proceedings at issue here, the lead prosecutor asked the local judge to refer the dismissal of charges to the supervising prosecutor (here, the provincial prosecutor) for ratification or revocation within 30 days, which the trial court did in its order issued December 10, 2015. *See* Proceeding No. 11313-2015-00435, *supra* note 4.

5. Trial Before the Criminal Court ("Segunda Instancia")

The Court of Criminal Guarantees took notice of the proceedings on January 12, 2016. Notice was provided as private petitioner to the Ministry of the Interior's Legal Coordinator,[154] who presented evidence and summoned more than 10 witnesses to the final trial hearing. At this stage, the private petitioner's intervention had increased, according to the court, to the point of inappropriately submitting a written "premature plea" prior the hearing.[155]

The private petitioner also appointed and authorized three attorneys to represent him in the proceedings and at the trial hearing. In addition, at the request of one of the parties (it can be inferred from the file that likely at the Office of the Attorney General's request), the Criminal Court summoned the Governor of Loja, who represents the executive branch in the Province, to participate at the trial hearing.

In all, 22 defendants proceeded to the trial phase before the Criminal Court, which summoned the first group of 10 defendants for a trial hearing that ended May 30, 2016.[156] At that hearing, the Criminal Court found two defendants guilty and acquitted the other eight. A summons for the remaining 12 defendants' trial remains pending.

---

154. The Criminal Court took notice following a drawing held on the 8th day of that month.

155. The Criminal Court remarked that "With regard to the preemptive written argument submitted by Dr. Diego Jose Torres Saldana, because is too far removed from the procedural formalities that correspond in this matter and contravenes the accusatorial adversarial principle, which includes the principles of orality and contradiction, it will not be considered." Proceeding No. 11313-2015-00435, before the Tribunal of Criminal Guarantees of the Province of Loja.

156. The Criminal Court summoned trial for March 21 to April 8, and later rescheduled it twice, to May 11–13 and May 25–June 11, 2016.

6. Excessive and Disproportionate Use of Force

Although it was known beforehand that the protest was political in nature, the Government and its provincial representatives did not address it that way. Rather, it was handled as a conflict and approached as a battle to be waged by the army and police, who subdued through force and strength a community engaged in protest, exercising its rights of assembly, demonstration, and resistance.

In the same vein, a clear command from above to reopen the road as quickly as possible can be detected, which provoked an immediate use of force without any opportunity for dialogue. Police carried out those orders employing excessive measures to accomplish its objective. Thus, they proceeded to clear the road where the protesters had gathered to protest. With no intention of negotiating, they immediately resorted to using force.

If the objective was merely to remove the protesters, different methods were available. Their withdrawal could even have been mediated through the appropriate decision-makers.

Moreover, the Army participated in the operation, whose mere presence constitutes a mechanism for intimidation. The soldiers, like the police, overwhelmed with their attire, clubs, shields, and tear gas grenades. Due to its harmful effects, the use of this and other gases should be limited to a last resort. Using those items vitiated the sanity and efficiency with which imposing order could have proceeded.

According to the version of facts presented in proceedings, the police and military used disproportionate force in arresting the Saraguro community members. The use of force was exaggerated, not only due to their use of weapons, but also because of the large number of personnel deployed along the road.

Police forces pursued the demonstrators toward the surrounding hills. In some cases, they entered homes and private land without any regard for private property or the privacy of the families residing there.

Excessive use of force can also be seen at the moment of making the arrests. There is no justification for swarming over those persons already succumbed to asphyxiation from the tear gas deployed along the road. The protesters were peasants and wore their daily attire. Even if a group of protesters had wielded sticks and stones, would not justify the exaggerated use of tear gas bombs.

The number Saraguro community members present along the road was small—some were even just passing through the area—and they were trapped in a bottleneck that had formed at the end of a dip in the road.

In many cases, arrests were made at random. Surely it was for this reason that the Court of Criminal Guarantees acknowledged the innocence of all but two of the first cohort of defendants tried. It is also worth remembering that the local prosecutor had likewise refrained from charging the second group of defendants later indicted by the provincial prosecutor.

7. Excessive Punishment for the Offenses Committed as a Threat Mechanism

The offense with which the defendants were charged is punishable by a prison sentence of 1-3 years.[157] As

---

157. COIP, *supra* note 5, art. 346 criminalizes the stoppage of a public service: "Any person who impairs, obstructs, or paralyzes the regular

described above, this crime consists of the stoppage of a public service. Strictly speaking, the conduct in question must meet all of the criminal elements in the definition of the offense—here, to impair, obstruct, or paralyze a public service, or to resist its restoration. In addition, an act must be identified that is culpable, unlawful, and statutorily defined as punishable. The defendants did not impair, obstruct, or paralyze a public service; accordingly, there was no act. The defined offense does not fit the defendants' conduct, because they set out to protest, not to paralyze any public service. The actions were not unlawful because the defendants exercised their constitutional rights to assembly, demonstration, and resistance.

The punishment for the crime of impairing, obstructing, or paralyzing a public service, or resisting its restoration is disproportionate in comparison to others defined in the Criminal Code; it can be seen that it exists as such for the purpose of repressing public demonstrations.

8. Constitutional Rights As a Check on Criminal Laws

The Constitution of Ecuador establishes the principle of progressivity of rights, which provides that they must always be applied for the benefit of the person who holds them. When two rules are at odds, the adjudicator (judge, court, or tribunal) must always seek to enforce the one that safeguards the individual's rights.

In the case at hand, the defendants' rights were applied regressively instead of progressively. Criminal

---

provision of a public service or violently resists the restoration thereof; or who takes a public building or facility by force; shall be punished by imprisonment for one to three years."

charges were filed against 29 citizens who participated in a protest and, according to the Attorney General's Office and the Police, engaged in the constitutionally forbidden act of stopping a public service, in this case public transit. According to the Comprehensive Organic Criminal Code (COIP), that forbidden act translates into the crime stoppage of public services, which is punishable by one to three years of imprisonment.

At the same time, there exists a constitutional right to "good living" (*buen vivir*), which according to the Constitution consists of the exercise of associating, gathering, and demonstrated in a free and voluntary manner.[158] In addition, the Constitution recognizes the right of groups and individuals to resist, in the face of possible or actual constitutional violations by government authorities.[159]

It is a matter of logic that these rights override in form and substance the charges leveled by the authorities, because they are guaranteed by the Constitution. If it were not allowable to publicly demonstrate, how could the aforementioned rights be exercised? By overcoming the prohibition on stopping public transit, the rights to assembly, demonstration, and resistance would be denied application and therefore be left toothless.

The Constitution provides that the recognition of rights must be performed progressively, and that its development shall be formalized by means of norms, public policies, and judicial precedents.[160] Moreover, it defines

---

158. CONSTITUCION, *supra* note 7, at art. 66(13).
159. *Id.* at art. 98. This right to resistance also applies to acts or omissions by natural or non-state legal entities that undermine or may undermine the group or individual's constitutional rights, and also secures the right to demand the recognition of new rights.
160. *Id.* at art. 11(8).

as the State's primary obligation to respect the rights guaranteed by the Constitution.[161]

In the case studied here and similar others, the legal analysis performed by the judicial authorities must be rooted in the arguments presented above. In applying justice, those principles should not be obviated in any instance.

The above implies the need to scrutinize constitutional law in order to avoid conflict between rights — such as, in this case, between the right to assemble for protest and the right to public transportation, keeping in mind the superiority and importance of the former.

9. International Law

We must refer not only to the constitutional principles described above, but also to the provisions of international law. Mainly, we must consider the rights to assembly, demonstration, resistance, and due process. Those rights are embedded in principles on which several international forums have weighed in.

The International Labor Organization, through its Committee on Freedom of Association, has stated that "No person should be detained for the mere fact of having participated in a demonstration, unless public order is seriously endangered."[162] Likewise, the Inter-American Commission on Human Rights has stated that "[t]he detention of participants in peaceful demonstrations

---

161. Additionally, it provides that when a criminal sentence is modified or revoked, the State must compensate the person who suffered at its expense, with liability and responsibility falling on the judicial servant who issued the sentence. *Id.* at art. 11(9), fifth paragraph.

162. INTERNATIONAL LABOUR OFFICE, DIGEST OF DECISIONS AND PRINCIPLES OF THE FREEDOM OF ASSOCIATION COMMITTEE para. 130 (4th ed. 1996).

violates freedom of assembly, even if deprivation of liberty lasts only some hours and does not result in a criminal charge."[163] This confirms the impermissibility of repressing the rights to assembly, demonstration, resistance.

With respect to judicial proceedings, international law provides that they should comply with minimum guarantees and proceed in conditions of absolute fairness. It insists that cases should be heard before independent and impartial tribunals that abide by and apply the principles of legality, due process, and judicial guarantees.[164]

In analyzing the case at hand, it is indispensable to consider the principle of judicial independence.[165] This principle assumes that judicial authorities are devoid of "any restrictions, improper influences, inducements, pressures, threats or interferences, direct or indirect, from any quarter or for any reason."[166] This implies the right to be heard before competent, independent, and impartial authorities.

---

163. OFFICE OF THE UNITED NATIONS HIGH COMMISSIONER FOR HUMAN RIGHTS, REGIONAL OFFICE FOR SOUTH AMERICA, INTERNATIONAL HUMAN RIGHTS LAW 693 (2007).

164. *See* Universal Declaration of Human Rights art. 10, G.A. Res. 217 (III) A, U.N. Doc. A/RES /217(III) (Dec. 10, 1948) *and* Organization of American States, American Convention on Human Rights art. 8, Nov. 22, 1969, O.A.S.T.S. No. 36, 1144 U.N.T.S. 123.

165. The principle of judicial independence is separate in its conception from that of the principle of judicial impartiality. According to the Inter-American Commission on Human Rights, "[i]mpartiality presumes that the court or judge do not have preconceived opinions about the case *sub judice* and, in particular, do not presume the accused to be guilty." Martin de Mejia v. Peru, Case 10.970, Inter. Am. Comm'n H.R., Report No. 5/96, OEA/Ser.L/V/II.91, doc. 7 ¶ 68 (1996).

166 Basic Principles on the Independence of the Judiciary art. 2, *endorsed by* G.A. Res. 40/32 (Nov. 29, 1985) *and* G.A. Res. 40/146 (Dec. 13, 1985).

The principle of independence also applies to the work of the Attorney General's Office, which must always act without interference, intimidation, obstruction, or harassment. Both Inter-American Human Rights tribunals have confirmed the applicability of the principle of due process, including the principles of independence and impartiality and the presumption of innocence, to the preliminary stages of a criminal proceeding.[167] In the case analyzed here, there appears to be a particular interest at work in making the charges stick, as evidenced by the provincial prosecutors revocation of the local prosecutors dismissal of most of the defendants' charges.

In the exercise of judicial authority, both during the criminal proceedings and in administering justice, necessary care must be taken to apply the facts to the statutory definition of the offense.

In this case, the conduct of those arrested during the demonstration does not coincide with the definition of the crime with which the prosecution charged them. With respect to this, the Inter-American Court on Human Rights has held that "it is incumbent upon the criminal judge, upon applying criminal law, to strictly abide by the provisions thereof and be extremely rigorous when likening the accused person's conduct to the criminal definition, so as not to punish someone for acts that are not punishable under the legal system."[168] In this case, due process

---

167. *See* Martin de Mejia, *supra* note 26, at ¶¶ 65–67 (1996).
168. Garcia Asto and Ramirez Rojas v. Peru, Preliminary Objection, Merits, Reparations and Costs, Inter. Am. Ct. H.R. (Ser. C) No. 137 ¶ 190 (Nov. 25, 2005). *See also* Fermin Ramirez v. Guatemala, Merits, Reparations, and Costs, Inter. Am. Ct. H.R. (Ser. C) No. 126 ¶ 90 (June 20, 2005) *and* Cruz Flores v. Peru, Merits, Reparations, and Costs, Inter. Am. Ct. H.R. (Ser. C) No. 115 ¶ 82 (Nov. 18, 2004).

was violated, infringing on the defendants' right to a fair and impartial hearing based on the facts presented in the proceedings.

Moreover, the principle of congruence must be considered, which requires coherence between the facts based on which the prosecution accuses, the defense presented by the accused, the evidence presented by the parties, and the reasoning and decision of the judge. The jurisprudence of the National Court of Justice has spoken favorably of this principle, emphasizing its value for the right to a proper defense and the logical structure of the proceedings.[169]

Likewise, in the case studied here, we saw an absence in the decisions of the judicial authorities of the indispensable legal reasoning required—particularly in the Attorney General's Office's anemic complaint and the trial court's bare-bones trial order. Ecuadorian constitutional law refers to three requirements for the verification of a judicial decision: reasonableness, logic, and comprehensibility.[170]

---

169. Judicial Gazette, Tribunal of the Criminal Chamber of the National Court of Justice, Ser. 18, No. 13 (Aug. 1, 2013) "In the new legal system, in which we find ourselves, the principle of congruence is important, that is, there should be a consonance between the statement of objections and the judgment, in order to guarantee the right to a defense, procedural fidelity, and also the legal and logical structure of the proceeding, since a defendant can only be convicted or acquitted for the charges for which he was called to respond. There must be congruence between the final punishment given to the accused and the specific facts that motivated the accusation, without introducing new facts on which the defendant could not defend himself. Consequently, there cannot be conviction for a different criminal offense, unless they are homogeneous or comparable offenses, and they protect the same legal good."

170. "Reasonableness" means that the judicial decision is based on constitutional, legal, and jurisprudential reasoning; "logic" refers to

The local judge's failed on all counts: he did not apply the constitutional principles of progressiveness of rights and of favorability; he held that the defendants stopped a public service, when in reality they were exercising their rights to assembly, demonstration, and resistance; and, its analysis is limited to a transcription of accounts with a very brief application of law to the facts.

10. Conclusion: Consequences for Democracy and Legal Security in Ecuador

The Ecuadorean Constitution recognizes the right to legal certainty, which implies the existence of previously defined, clear, and public rules, applied by competent authorities. This is a characteristic of a State of Rights. An essential aspect in this regard is the tangible presence of a clear separation of functions and respect for competencies.

Ecuador must bring to bear the ancient principles of a republican democracy, whose citizens may exercise their rights effectively. To this end, a judicial and institutional order is required that grants absolute practical guarantees for the application of an absolute—that is, respected and recognized—judicial independence.

It is crucial to discard the malicious prosecution of criminal charges or proceedings as a means of social intimidation, typically for political ends and with the idea in mind of setting precedents that illustrate the scope of state power.

In the case analyzed here reveals a lack of respect for—or worse, absence of—judicial autonomy, due to

coherence between analysis, inferences, and decisions; and "comprehensibility" refers to wording that is given to clear understanding.

influence in judicial decisions by authorities at all levels. That situation leaves few options for those expecting in prosecutors, judges, tribunals, and courts an authority that exclusively rules based on the law, and not to advance the interests of any third parties. Behind this case, we can see the government's intention to impose a punishment to make a public example, at the expense of a judicial system that instills confidence in the citizenry.

VI
THE RELATIONSHIP BETWEEN GOVERNMENT AND CIVIL SOCIETY, AND THE ABUSE OF CRIMINAL LAW IN ECUADOR

Sebastian Gonzalez[171]
Pier Pigozzi[172]

I. Executive Summary

This study analyzes the persecution of actual or perceived opposition, criminalization of social protest, and lack of judicial independence in Ecuador, through a case study of the criminal prosecution of student demonstrators at the *Colegio Central Técnico* school. This was yet another case in which President Rafael Correa Delgado made public statements in his weekly address to the nation criticizing the performance of judges and prosecutors—in this case, for acquitting 12 high school students who took part in a protest against the Ministry of Education's decision to change the name of their school. Following the President's public intervention, what had until then been a mere student protest was re-cast as a crime of rebellion. The prosecution withdrew its dismissal of charges against the students, and criminal proceedings against them were set initiated that lacked impartiality and vio-

---

171. Attorney, Pontifical Catholic University of Ecuador (2007). Specialist in Constitutional and Electoral Law, Externado University of Colombia (2011).
172. Attorney, Pontifical Catholic University of Ecuador (2007). LL.M. (2010) and J.S.D. candidate, Notre Dame School of Law. Law Professor, San Francisco de Quito University.

lated the students' due process and fundamental rights. The case shows that President Correa's government is willing to instigate judicial persecution not only to intimidate high-profile political opponents, but also as a weapon in random cases — without regard for the targets' youth or lack of any public or political profile, or to existing prosecutorial and judicial decisions that had already determined their innocence.

II. The Case of the *Colegio Central Técnico* Students

The National Police on February 22, 2013, arrested 12 adult students of the *Colegio Central Técnico* school while they protested among 600 other students against the Ministry of Education's decision to change their school's name to *Unidad Educativa Temporal Central Tecnico*. The arrest was made based on a police report that did not identify which among the 600 protesting students were allegedly responsible for damaging public and private property or for assailing police officers.

After the events, Vice Minister of Education Adminiatration Monica Franco said in an interview that the protesting students had been manipulated by "strange forces" with the purpose of destabilizing the government.[173] At the arraignment, prosecutors requested the pretrial detention of the students and their trial for the crime of rebellion. At the pretrial hearing held pursuant to the criminal procedural rules on March 28, 2013, the designated prosecutor decided not to charge the 12 students

---

173. *See* Guevara, Leonardo, raicestv, *67 estudiantes detenidos en Quito, ministerio de educacion, raices tv* [*67 students detained in Quito, ministry of education, raices tv*], YouTube (Feb. 25, 2013), https://www.youtube.com/watch?v=CWP4gnvxVEI., at 1:20.

due to lack of evidence of the crime with which they were charged[174] — a decision shared by the judge of the Judicial Unit of Criminal Guarantees.[175]

Two days later, however, President Correa, in national address number 315,[176] referred to the case and openly criticized the prosecution and the judge.[177] In this statement, he assumed the role of appellate court, engaging in an incriminatory assessment of the videos and photos taken on the day of the student protest.[178] He repeatedly insisted that justice operators were intimidated by media pressure into not prosecuting the students; that what

174. *See* Minutes, Pretrial Hearing and Substantiation of Prosecutor's Petition, Case 2013-0508. Bormman Penaherrera, the prosecutor, stated at that hearing: "[B]ased on the videos, none of the 12 detainees can be observed performing acts of rebellion. There is no record of destruction of public, private, or police property; and none of the students carried firearms ... [accordingly,] there are sufficient elements for the prosecution to refrain from pressing charges."

175. At the hearing, the judge ordered "provisional dismissal of the proceedings and final dismissal of the accused." *Id.*

176. These addresses to the nation are the platform implemented by the government to report back to the Ecuadorian people on the state of the nation's public affairs. They are available on the government's official website at http://enlaceciudadano.gob.ec.

177. The President of the Republic said: "[T]he prosecutor says there are no guilty parties — play the video — so they were robots, all these spoiled kids were robots.... [K]now how to assign responsibility where it is due, the President is not the culprit here.... [T]his was no social protest, gentlemen, these are criminals." He continued: "We respect the decision of the Judge and the Prosecutor very much, but we absolutely do not share it. We believe they have allowed themselves be controlled by the press." Presidencia de la Republica del Ecuador, *Enlace Ciudadano Nro 315 desde Olmedo – Manabi*, YOUTUBE (Mar. 30, 2103), https://www.youtube.com/watch?feature =player_ embedded&v=hwZGqDVqg5M, at 2:32:35.

178. The President said "Mr. Prosecutor, I am sending you the videos so that you have no remaining doubts about who threw the stones.... [T]his will be appealed because adults should be punished.... [T]hey can not be completely absolved..... I hope prosecutors and judges do not let themselves be so easily intimidated; here they were intimidated by so much public pressure." *Id.* at 2:34:24.

happened at the school was not a mere social protest, but instead was the work of criminals; and that so long as he remains president, he would not allow that sort of behavior from "wayward youths" ("*muchachos desubicados*").[179]

Faced with those statements, the prosecutor for the Province of Pichincha decided two days later to withdraw the dismissal of charges and called the 12 students[180] to trial with a ruling unsupported by any legal reasoning.[181] On September 4, 2013, the 12 *Colegio Central Tecnico* students were convicted as principals in the crime of rebellion.[182] The conviction was ratified on appeal by the Criminal Chamber of the Provincial Court of Justice of Pichincha and by the Criminal, Military Criminal, Police Criminal, and Transit Chambers of the National Court of Justice, which denied the appeal and cassation appeal, respectively.[183]

The case of the *Central Tecnico* students marks the start of a repeated practice by the government of criminalizing

---

179. *Id.* at 2:33:06.

180 The statute in effect at the time, Code of Criminal Procedure article 226, provided that, because a crime against the public administration was at issue, if the prosecutor declined to press charges, that dismissal had to be presented to a supervising prosecutor for ratification. Here, however, the senior prosecutor did not wait for the case to be submitted for review, and instead withdrew the case prosecutor's dismissal *sua sponte*. *See* Order, Case No. 2013-0508.

181. Order No. [*NB: This order has been requested in writing from the prosecution, but the government has denied access to the case files.*]

182 *See* Judgment of June 12, 2013. Dr. Nelson de la Cadena Galarza, judge in the Pichincha Criminal Guarantees Unit of Pichincha, stated there that "there are serious and well-founded presumptions about the existence of the crime and the participation of those indicted as principals in the crime of rebellion."

183. Judgment of May 8, 2014, issued by Associate Justices ("*Conjueces Nacionales*") Alejandro Arteaga Garcia and Richard Villagomez Cabezas.

students who protest on the streets, accusing them of destabilizing the regime and of being beholden to the interests of certain political leaders.[184] The case also illustrates how the President of the Republic corrupts the decisions of the judiciary with the consent and complicity of the Judiciary Council.[185]

III. Intrusion by the Ecuadorean Executive Power Into Judicial Decision-Making

In principle, one of the main axes of President Correa's governance plan was to restructure the judiciary.[186] The

---

184. The Ecumenical Commission on Human Rights of Ecuador expressed its concern in a September 26, 2014, press release about the situation of several students of the *Colegio Mejia* school who were detained for allegedly damaging third-party personal property, and also stressed the lack of legal reasoning in the judge and prosecutor's decisions. Another press release describes the arbitrary detention of a group of students from the *Colegio Montufar* school, who were detained on February 15, 2016, without any charge or report that specifically named any individual suspects. Press Release, Comision Ecumenica de Derechos Humanos, *Manifestacion juvenil dejo varios heridos y detenidos* [Youth Protest Leaves Several Wounded and Detained] (Feb. 18, 2016), *available at* http://www.cedhu.org/ index.php? option=com_content& view=article&id=430:2016-02-24-01-25-28&catid= 24:noticias-anteriores.

185. Judiciary Council President Gustavo Jalk said that "everyone has an opinion on the judiciary." Specifically regarding the *Central Tecnico* case, he maintained that, in his opinion, there was no interference by the executive branch in the judiciary. RTU Noticias, *Continua polemica por liberacion de estudiantes del Central Tecnico* [Controversy Continues over Release of Central Tecnico Students] YouTube (Apr. 13, 2013), https://www.youtube.com/watch?v=TfUgzBLiU_8, at 0:58.

186. In several public statements, the President has insisted on the need to reform the justice system, even stating that he would "meddle with" the judiciary. Presidencia de la Republica del Ecuador, *Enlace Ciudadano Nro 203 desde Baeza – Napo*, YouTube (June 18, 2014), https:// www. youtube.com/watch?feature=player_ embedded&v=hwZGq-DVqg5M, at 88:00.

adoption of the new Constitution—passed in 2008[187] and ratified in the May 2011 referendum process—that set out to invest the judiciary with a strengthened and renovated Judicial Council was the most significant change ever in the country's justice system, and was promised to provide us the most independent and impartial judiciary yet. In practice, however, the opposite happened. The reforms gave rise to more frequent—and more scandalous, even—executive intrusion into judicial matters. In practice, the yielding of judicial power to executive interests operates in two ways. One is external, and arises through pressures exercised by the executive through various spheres of power—as illustrated by the case at hand, where by holding the judge and prosecutor up to criticism and ridicule in a public speech, the executive made known to them that the disposition of the case should be changed. The other is internal, in that the excessive disciplinary controls to which judges and prosecutors are subject translate into sanctions and dismissal for the justice operators who do not conform their rulings to the government's whims.

The year 2013 was marked by a string of cases involving similar abuses committed against legislators, advisors, political party leaders, and indigenous leaders.[188] In

187. Judicial independence is a fundamental principle of the Ecuadorean Constitution. *See* Constitucion de la Republica de Ecuador art. 168.1 (2008) ("The administration of justice, in compliance with its duties and in the exercise of its attributions, shall apply the following principles: 1. The bodies of the Judicial Branch shall benefit from both internal and external independence. Any breach of this principle shall entail administrative, civil, and criminal liability, in accordance with the law." To that end, the Constitution in article 178 reserves to the Judicial Council the function of directing the administration of justice.

188. *See* Basabe Serrano, Santiago and Martinez, Julian, *Cada vez menos democracia, cada vez mas autoritarismo ... con elecciones* [Each

126

the case of the *Colegio Central Tecnico* students, the president clearly adopted the role of examiner of judicial decisions in order to persecute the youths, indiscriminately wielding the criminal system to silence their speaking out. In doing so, the government set a clear precedent: that all protests can be punished with arrest and prosecution for the offense of rebellion[189] — even if they only involve students — under the arbitrary justification that they create chaos and destabilize the government. The students' fundamental human rights to freedom of association, protest, and expression were seriously infringed by the abusive exercise of a political power that directly controls, supervises, and influences the decisions of the administrators of judicial institutions.

IV. Lack of Judicial Independence and the Ensuing Human Rights Violations

According to the Inter-American Commission on Human Rights, "[t]he independence of any body or organ that performs jurisdictional functions is a condition *sine qua non* for the observance of the standards of due process as a human right."[190] Accordingly, we can assert that, in a true democratic state, judicial independence ensures the effective enjoyment of the right of access to justice, gener-

---

TIME LESS DEMOCRACY, AND EACH TIME MORE AUTHORITARIANISM ... WITH ELECTIONS], 34 REVISTA DE CIENCIAS POLÍTICAS 145, 155-56 (2014).

189. The current criminal statute defines rebellion as follows: "Any person who rebels or performs violent actions whose objective is the repeal of Constitution of the Republic or the overthrow of the legitimately constituted government (without affecting the legitimate right to resistance) shall be punished with the penalty of deprivation of liberty for five to seven years...." CODIGO ORGANICO INTEGRAL PENAL art. 336 (2014).

190. Inter-Am. Comm'n H.R., *Guarantees for the independence of justice operators*, at ¶ 30, OEA/Ser.L/V/II., doc. 44 (Dec. 5 2003).

ating confidence among citizens that any arbitrary exercise of power will be reviewed by the courts.

On the other hand, the absence of this guarantee—translating into an almost absolute dependence by the judicial branch on the executive—encourages a climate of human rights abuses, and generates distrust and even fear among citizens from asserting their rights before the courts. The United Nations Human Rights Committee has clearly stated that "[a] situation where the functions and competencies of the judiciary and the executive are not clearly distinguishable or where the latter is able to control or direct the former is incompatible with the notion of an independent tribunal."[191] An independent tribunal is one of the main purposes of the separation of powers, and a foundational pillar of due process.[192]

As has been documented in recent years,[193] the executive power in Ecuador has constantly interfered with the courts and even legitimized "meddling with the

---

191. U.N. Human Rights Comm'n,, *Article 14. Right to equality before courts and tribunals and to fair trial,* ¶ 30, U.N. Doc. CCPR/C/GC/32 (Aug. 23, 2007).

192. *See* Constitutional Court v. Peru, Merits, Reparations, and Costs, Judgment, Inter-Am. Ct. H.R. (Ser. C) No. 71, ¶¶ 73 and 75 (Jan. 31, 2001).

193. For example, the International Observatory of the Judicial Reform in Ecuador recommended in its final report that "respect and non-interference from the other branches of government with the Judiciary should be guaranteed. The separation of powers should be not only a theory, but an absolute reality." Veeduria Internacional, Informe Final de la Veeduria Internacional a la Reforma de la Justicia en Ecuador 15 (2005). Another study similarly concluded that "the pattern established in this country is that, each time that those governing required some judicial decision that the judges were not willing to issue, [the judges] were relieved of their charges." Pasara, Luis, Due Process of Law Found., Independencia judicial en la reforma de la justicia ecuatoriana 92 (July 28, 2014), *available at* http://www.dplf.org/sites/default/files/indjud_ecuador_informe_esp.pdf.

judiciary" ("*metida de manos en la justicia*"), in the words of President Correa himself. Under the pretense of correcting and amending judgments that he deems incompatible with the principles of the so-called "citizens' revolution,"[194] the president plays the role of prosecutor and judge by handing down orders through public speeches, without any minimum guarantee of legality, and without the fundamental rights of any person effectively limiting his power.

In the *Colegio Tecnico* case and in student protest cases that followed, in taking to the streets in protest, the students exercised their right to freedom of expression and assembly—both fully recognized under the Constitution.[195] Both rights were infringed, first, not only by the police forces that detained them without real justification, but also by the criminal proceedings to which they were subjected, which lacked any due process protections or even the basic guarantee of being heard by an independent and impartial judge. Secondly, the notoriety given to the case exposed the students' names to public opinion and injured their dignity and reputation and that of their relatives.

Those actions clearly violate the human rights enshrined in the American Convention on Human Rights,

---

194. "Public statements by political authorities regarding the performance of judges suggest that the problem facing judicial independence in Ecuador is not a legal issue, but a political one." PASARA, at 94.
195. CONSTITUCION, *supra* note 17, at arts. 66(6) and 66(13), respectively. *See also* Inter-Am. Comm'n H.R., Annual Report of the Office of the Special Rapporteur for Freedom of Expression 2005, ch. V, at ¶ 6, OEA/Ser.L/V/II.124, doc. 27 (Feb. 27, 2006) ("[T]he right to demonstrate is protected both by the right to freedom of expression and by the right to freedom of assembly.").

namely, the rights to be heard by an impartial tribunal,[196] the right to an effective recourse for protection against acts that violate fundamental rights,[197] the right to freedom of thought and expression,[198] the right of assembly,[199] and the right to honor and dignity.[200]

These violations stemming from executive interference in judicial decision-making does not only prevent the persons subject to judicial proceedings from exercising their fundamental rights. They also have the effect of intimidating society as a whole, because there is no effective system of democratic checks and balances to defend against acts of political persecution by the ruling administration. The role of judges in a democratic system, according to the Inter-American Commission on Human Rights, must be to "ensure that the acts of other branches of government and public servants in general are consistent with the conventions to which the State is party and with its constitution and laws."[201]

V. Conclusions

The case of the *Colegio Central Técnico* students brings to light the Correa administration's regular practice of using official discourse to meddle in judicial decisions. This mechanism of intimidation is exerted not only on judges but also on prosecutors, with the complicity of the Judicial Council.

---

196. Organization of American States, American Convention on Human Rights art. 8.1, Nov. 22, 1969, O.A.S.T.S. No. 36, 1144 U.N.T.S. 123.
197. *Id.* at art. 25.
198. *Id.* at art. 13.1.
199. *Id.* at art. 15.
200. *Id.* at art. 11.
201. Guarantees, *supra* note 20, at ¶ 16.

The constitutional rights of students to freedom of thought and expression have been drastically curtailed. Based on the government's theory that every student protest is politically motivated and seeks to destabilize the regime, police force is used to indiscriminately detain and criminalize any student who participates in a protest. This case shows that a subjective and incomplete police report that fails to identify the alleged perpetrators is enough to detain anyone and subject him or her to criminal prosecution without due process protections or judicial impartiality and independence.

The guarantee of judicial independence enshrined in the Constitution does not exist in practice. Cases abound of judges and prosecutors punished for not complying with orders issuing from the Executive, according to various studies as well as international observers of the judiciary reform process in Ecuador.[202] The lack of judicial independence in Ecuador, with the resulting persecution of students, punishment of judges and prosecutors, criminalization of social protest, and violation of human rights in criminal proceedings, all clash with and undermine one of the fundamental tenets of any democracy — the doctrine of separation of powers.

This case marks the start of a systematic persecution of students who engage in protest; however, the current government has also shown its willingness to prosecute opponents and criminalize protest in other contexts, as well. What is particularly alarming about this case of judicial persecution is that the targets were not opposition candidates or legislators, whose actions might have some

---

202. *See, e.g.*, Informe Final, *supra* note 24.

potential to diminish the hitherto absolute power of Rafael Correa's government.[203] Here, the persecution by the government reached citizens who lacked the political or economic power to cause any meaningful impact against the regime. This protest by 600 students was about something as intimate (and trivial, in terms of the country's overall political affairs) as the name of their school.

Even before this case, it was clear that the abuse of political power by Rafael Correa's government knows no limits in the constitution, let alone the law. From this case, we now know that government repression also knows no limits in the relevance of the protest, the age of the alleged participants, nor the impact (or, as here, lack thereof) that a dissident's words or actions may have on national affairs. The Ecuadorean government is willing to persecute anyone, for any reason or for no reason—even the weakest among us.

---

203. As had been the case in previous cases of persecution, such as those reported by Santiago Basabe and Julian Martinez. *See* CADA VEZ MENOS, *supra* note 18.

INTRODUCTION. Ambassador Armando Valladares is a painter, poet and writer. He spent 22 years in political prisons in Cuba. Valladares received the Freedom Prize of the Pen Club. Was adopted by Amnesty International as a prisoner of conscience, then French president François Mitterrand asked Castro for his freedom. Ronald Reagan, after reading his memoirs of prison *Against All Hope*, named him U.S. Ambassador to the UN Commission on Human Rights. He obtained the condemnation of Cuba for the violation of these rights, for which he received the Presidential Medal of the Citizen, the second most important award that a civilian in the United States can receive. Also the Superior Award is the highest distinction awarded by the State Department to diplomats. Armando received the Truman-Reagan Freedom Medal given to victims of Communism. For his unconditional defense of freedom of conscience, he received the Canterbury Medal in 2016, the highest honor given by the Becket Fund for Religious Liberty. He was Chairman of the Human Rigths Foundation based in New York. In addition to leading the human rights committee of the Interamerican Institute for Democracy (IID), he also has the Valladares Foundation which defends children's rights. He is the author of *El Alma de un poeta* (The Soul of a Poet), *Desde mi Silla de Ruedas* (From my Wheelchair), *El Corazón Con Que Vivo* (The Heart with which I Live), *Cavernas del Silencio* (Caverns of Silence) and the Best Seller *Contra toda Esperanza* (Against All Hope).

PROLOGUE: Inter-American Bar Association - Prof. Bjorn Arp Ph.D. Dr. Björn Arp is a Fellow at American University Washington College of Law Center on International Commercial Arbitration where he also co-teaches International Commercial Arbitration. He is also editor-in-chief of the Law of the Sea Reports and a partner at Aparicio, Arp & Associates LLC, in Washington, D.C. He taught Public International Law, European Union Law, and Investment Arbitration at the University of Alcalá, Madrid, from 2000 to 2010. In 2007, Arp was a visiting researcher at Harvard Law School. His publications and researches have focused on International Investment Protection and Human Rights

PRESENTATION: Prof. Douglas Cassel J.D. Professor Cassel is a distinguished and widely published scholar, attorney and commentator specialized in International Human Rights Law, especially regarding to issues of Business and Human Rights, regional Human Rights Systems, International Criminal and Humanitarian Law. He is the President of the Board of the Justice Studies Center of the Americas, to which he has been elected three times by the Organization of American States, and former President of the Due Process of Law Foundation. He has served as a consultant on Human Rights to the United Nations, Organization of American States, United States Department of State and Department of Justice, the Ford Foundation, and numerous non-governmental human rights organizations. He lectures worldwide and his articles are published internationally in both English and Spanish.

Forum "The Role of the Judiciary in the Violation of Human Rights in Ecuador"

Björn Arp, Beatrice Rangel, Douglass Cassel, Juan Antonio Blanco and Congresswoman: Ileana Ros-Lehtinen.

Carlos Sánchez Berzaín, Rafael Paredes, Douglass Cassel, Jorge Zavala Egas, Francisco Endara, Beatrice Rangel, Congresista: Ileana Ros-Lehtinen, Björn Arp, Jaime Vintimilla, Daniela Salazar, Fabricio Rubianes Morales, Carlos Manosalvas.